Beyond the Xs and Os

Beyond the Xs and Os

Keeping the Bills in Buffalo

MARK C. POLONCARZ

excelsior editions

AN IMPRINT OF STATE UNIVERSITY OF NEW YORK PRESS

Cover image of the stadium from Wikimedia.

Published by State University of New York Press, Albany

Excelsior Editions is an imprint of State University of New York Press.

For information, contact State University of New York Press, Albany, NY
www.sunypress.edu

Library of Congress Cataloging-in-Publication Data

Names: Poloncarz, Mark C., 1967– author.
Title: Beyond the Xs and Os : keeping the Bills in Buffalo / Mark C. Poloncarz.
Description: Albany : Excelsior Editions ; State University of New York
  Press, [2019] | Includes bibliographical references and index.
Identifiers: LCCN 2018045849 | ISBN 9781438475936 (hardcover : alk. paper) |
  ISBN 9781438475950 (ebook)
Subjects: LCSH: Buffalo Bills (Football team)—History. | Football stadiums—
  New York (State)—Buffalo—History. | Football—Economic aspects—New York
  (State)—Buffalo. | Sports and state—New York (State)—Buffalo. | Poloncarz,
  Mark C., 1967–
Classification: LCC GV956.B83 P65 2019 | DDC 796.332/640974797—dc23
LC record available at https://lccn.loc.gov/2018045849

10 9 8 7 6 5 4 3 2 1

*This book is dedicated to
the fans of the Buffalo Bills.*

Contents

Prologue

I cannot tell you from memory the final score of the first Buffalo Bills' game I attended, nor can I recall who scored touchdowns for the Bills that day, but I do *remember* attending my first game.

Just like every other boy in my hometown of Lackawanna, New York, I was a Buffalo Bills fan. Joe Ferguson was the quarterback of my childhood memories. O.J. Simpson—not yet the sad, sordid person he'd later become—was the best running back in the National Football League. O.J. wore number 32. I was seven years old when my father turned thirty-two years of age. It seemed to me only the best running backs wore number 32. So when my father turned the same age as O.J.'s number I knew it meant something special because only the best get to be 32.

I watched every game I could and for years pestered my father to take me to my first game. Finally, in 1980, when I was just shy of my thirteenth birthday, my dad told me we were going to my first Bills game that fall. I knew this would be an experience I would never forget. And I never have.

We were playing our conference rivals the New York Jets. It was a beautiful day in early fall, the sun shining brightly. My dad told me to make sure I brought my football with me so we could toss it around before the game. While on the drive to Rich Stadium he said he was going to stop off at the store before we got to the game to pick up some food and drink for tailgating in the parking lot. I vividly remember wondering, "What is tailgating? And what does it have to do with watching the Bills game?"

It didn't take long for me to understand that attending a Buffalo Bills football game meant more than just watching the game. It meant grilling hot dogs and hamburgers in the parking lot before game time, playing touch football with other fans, and then entering Rich Stadium, a hulking behemoth. It meant sitting five rows from the top (I clearly remember that because I counted how close we were) and looking out and seeing eighty thousand fans, more people than I had ever seen in any one place—all there, like me, to watch the Bills.

It meant watching Joe Ferguson throw the ball to Jerry Butler and hand it off to Joe Cribbs or Roland Hooks. It meant hearing the Bills fans taunt the Jets fans and vice versa (including both sides saying a few off-color words I was not allowed to use). It meant watching Fred Smerlas and the rest of the "Bermuda Triangle" swallow up running backs who dared come up the middle. And ultimately, it meant leaving the game with a smile on my face after the Bills posted a 20 to 10 victory.

Of the years that followed, many of my most vivid memories revolve around Bills wins and losses: lying on my parents' couch with an icepack after hurting my knee playing street football, watching the Bills beat the Denver Broncos on a last-second field goal by Nick Mike-Mayer; sitting through the dismal sleet and cold rain of another loss during the back-to-back 2–14 seasons in the mid-'80s; driving to Cleveland's old Municipal Stadium to watch the playoff game in which Ronnie Harmon let the winning touchdown pass from Jim Kelly slip through his hands, thereby ending the Bills 1989–90 season (yes, I was there, in that end zone, and the pass went *right through* his hands); attending a Super Bowl XXV party at the West Seneca Moose Lodge where everyone was absolutely silent, holding hands, as Scott Norwood lined up the kick that every Bills' fan will remember him for.

Each of us who bleed Buffalo Bills red, white, and blue have these memories, these shared fan experiences. And when it comes to attending a game at Ralph Wilson Stadium, it is the entirety of the fan experience that makes it more than just a Sunday afternoon spent watching football, but a communal event all Bills fans have shared since Ralph C. Wilson, Jr. placed his team in Buffalo in 1959. It is that experience of being Bills fans that binds us together as western New Yorkers through the good and bad times that mark the history of our region.

Little did I imagine on that bright Sunday in 1980 that more than three decades later I would be involved in another type of game involving the Buffalo Bills—a game that could decide whether the team I grew up loving and, all too often, agonizing over would still call Buffalo home. But when I was elected Erie County's eighth county executive on November 8, 2011, I knew my legacy would be linked to one particular transaction: whether I could negotiate a new long-term lease to keep the Bills in Buffalo and continue building on what had been the region's cultural foundation for the better part of the last century.

When the people of Erie County gave me the privilege to serve as their county executive, I knew the task at hand would prove difficult. Having served six years as Erie County Comptroller, I was more than prepared to take on the position. I knew Erie County's finances like the back of my hand. I believed I was elected to restore government to its core principle, to serve its constituents, and I felt I had the support of those constituents to do so.

Yet, I knew no matter what I accomplished, my administration would be measured by our ability to successfully complete a new lease transaction with the Buffalo Bills. Even if I succeeded in every other goal of my administration—helped to rebuild our economy and grow our population—I knew if I failed to close a new lease transaction with the Bills and the team left for greener pastures, my administration would be deemed a failure.

The effort to complete that challenging task started almost immediately after I walked off the stage at the Adam's Mark Hotel on election night in 2011. When I left the stage, I turned and told my staff that if they thought winning the election was the hard part, they were wrong—the hard part had just begun.

This book is the story of how getting a long-term lease negotiated and signed by Erie County, New York State, and the Buffalo Bills proved to be an extremely difficult but ultimately very rewarding task. It is also the story of how our administration was able to navigate the turbulent waters bound to drown any negotiation by a billion-dollar football team, a county that owns the stadium where the team plays, and the fourth-most populous state in the country, all the while dealing almost daily with the local media's feeding frenzy for news.

The following narrative about the Bills negotiation is based on my memory, my written notes of meetings and phone conferences (including the exact words used by parties as written in my contemporaneous notes), letters exchanged by the parties, as well as hundreds and hundreds of emails between the parties. Any spelling or grammatical errors contained in the original letters or emails are included here without alteration.

In a transaction as complex as the Bills lease was and continues to be, many people were involved in making it a reality, but in my view none was more important than my former Deputy County Executive, Richard Tobe. Rich was Erie County's Commissioner of Environment and Planning during County Executive Dennis Gorski's administration and, more important, he was County Executive Gorski's main negotiator during the 1998 lease agreement. Rich's institutional knowledge of the previous lease terms proved invaluable during our efforts to secure a new lease. He spent countless hours as my chief negotiator during the process, always keeping me apprised of developments. We would often sit together and discuss the current status of negotiations, strategize possible outcomes, and work together to determine the county's desired course of action. I owe Rich a debt of gratitude for the time and effort he put in on the community's behalf.

I believe we as a community owe the late Ralph C. Wilson, Jr. a debt of gratitude as well. None of us would have had the pleasure of being Bills fans without his decision to place the team in Buffalo in 1959, and then to keep the team here when he could have moved it to much more lucrative pastures. I believe he knew he would not be alive to see the end of the lease we negotiated in 2012–13. By agreeing to the ironclad non-relocation terms demanded by the county and state to be included as part of the lease, Mr. Wilson knew he was setting the stage for the next owner to keep the team in Buffalo. While he may no longer be with us, the memory of Mr. Wilson's actions will live on for as long as the Bills are the Buffalo Bills.

Chapter 1

The Stadium in Orchard Park and the 1998 Lease Agreement

While the history of the Buffalo Bills dates back to the late 1950s when Mr. Ralph Wilson placed his team in Buffalo, Erie County's history with the team started a decade later. In the late 1960s, discussions in the community began regarding the building of a new football stadium to replace the old "Rockpile" at the corner of Best Street and Jefferson Avenue in Buffalo.

The history of what eventually resulted in the construction of Ralph Wilson Stadium could be the subject of a book in and of itself: from the announcement of the construction of a domed stadium in Lancaster, to allegations of corruption and graft by county legislators that led to the abandonment of that plan (and the eventual convictions of two county legislators on bribery charges), to the eventual selection in 1971 of approximately two hundred acres of vacant land on Abbott Road in Orchard Park as the location for a stadium, and finally to the construction of an eighty-thousand-seat, open-air stadium at the cost of $23 million—at the time, an astronomical sum.

When county executive B. John Tutuska and Bills owner Ralph C. Wilson signed a twenty-five-year lease for the new municipal stadium (soon to be named Rich Stadium after Erie County sold the naming rights to Rich Products), a long-term relationship began that would eventually result in my administration's efforts to negotiate a new lease in 2012 and 2013. Back then, though, the new stadium was a state-of-the-art facility that was different from the other facilities being built at the time. It was designed for football *only*, it was open to the air—not domed—and it could hold many more people than other stadiums constructed during that era. Other than Kansas City and Buffalo, most cities were building dual-purpose stadiums, some of which were domed, that held approximately 65,000 seats.

The true benefit of the choice of stadium is clear today: nearly every other stadium built at the time has since been replaced, with most of the original facilities demolished (think of Houston's Astrodome, Seattle's Kingdome, Cincinnati's Riverfront Stadium, and Pittsburgh's Three Rivers Stadium, just to name a few). Their replacements occurred not just because these cities wanted to build new facilities, but because the configuration of most domed or dual-purpose stadiums made major renovations to these facilities impractical. Any significant alteration to these stadiums was rendered almost impossible by their rounded design or dome, and every single one of these facilities no longer exists.

From this era, only Arrowhead Stadium in Kansas City and Ralph Wilson Stadium in Orchard Park remain. It is no coincidence that both of these facilities are similar in design: open-air, single-purpose facilities dedicated to football. Each could accommodate major renovations without destroying the structural integrity of the stadium.

The same can be said of two other older stadiums that recently underwent major renovations: Chicago's Soldier Field and Green Bay's Lambeau Field. While Soldier Field and Lambeau are significantly older than the Wilson and Arrowhead stadiums, both were designed as single-purpose, open-air stadiums that made a renovation or major retrofit economically viable.

The design of Ralph Wilson Stadium makes for one of the best features of attending a game there: you won't find a bad seat in the house. Ralph Wilson Stadium is known for having the best sightlines of any stadium in the NFL. The seats are much closer to the action than other stadiums, with no obstructed views, and offer a panoramic view of the entire facility. When I attended my first Bills game at age twelve, even though I was five rows from the top, I did not feel too far away to watch the action, and I clearly remember being mesmerized by both the facility and the fans.

On top of all this, the vast majority of the stadium, including the entire lower bowl, is below grade and built on top of shale bedrock. While this might not much impress the average fan in the seat, it means a tremendous amount regarding the structural integrity of the stadium. Although the stadium is nearing its forty-sixth year of continuous operation, its concrete and steel skeleton remain in great shape. In fact, based on assessments from the Erie County Department of Public Works, the stadium could last another twenty-five to thirty years before its structural integrity is compromised.

The primary reason is that the stadium was built fifty feet into the ground and on top of the local shale bedrock base. As a result, the vast majority of the infrastructure at the base of the stadium is sheltered from weather conditions by the ground, and the bedrock forms an extremely stable base without much movement or exposure to the elements. All in all, the engineers and designers hit a home run—or, rather, they threw and caught a ninety-nine-yard touchdown pass—when they designed the facility. It has survived more than forty winters very well, and probably much better than if it had been built at grade on top of dirt rather than fifty feet below grade on shale.

Another feature that leads to the incredible game-day experience at Ralph Wilson Stadium is the ample parking nearby, which makes for one of the best tailgating venues anywhere in the country, be it for professional or college football.

The County did not necessarily do this out of the kindness of its heart. The County owns all of the lots on the east side of Abbott Road between Southwestern Boulevard and Big Tree Road. It also owns the lots on the west side of the road, with those lots abutting Erie Community College's south campus. During the initial lease of twenty-five years, the County controlled the parking lots and benefitted from this term as it collected the revenue generated from parking. This was negotiated away during the 1998 lease renewal, but was a beneficial feature to the County for the first twenty-five years and helped to pay for the initial debt service construction costs of $23 million plus interest.

Prior to the 1998 lease, Erie County generated revenue from a variety of sources at the stadium. It sold the naming rights to the stadium to Rich Products. It generated revenue through contracts for the concession rights. It controlled the parking lots and shared in parking revenue and sold rights to private vendors to sell merchandise in the lots. All of this provided a nice revenue stream for the County, at least until the 1998 lease extension was signed.

Entering the last year of the first twenty-five-year lease agreement, County Executive Dennis Gorski was in a position similar to mine in 2012: no matter what he did otherwise, if the Bills moved, he would be blamed for the loss of the team. And to complicate matters, the NFL of 1997–98 was not the NFL of 1973. The league had progressed from being one of four major professional sports to being *the* major professional sport, with revenues generated from many sources unanticipated in 1973.

During the first twenty-five years of the stadium's existence, a number of major additions to the stadium and its surrounding campus occurred. Some of these, like the field house and the grass practice facility, were done to make the team more competitive on the field. A few were intended to assist the fans, such as restroom additions and the construction of a new parking lot. Others, such as the suites on the west side of the stadium and the "Red Zone/Goal Line" clubs, were designed to make the team more economically viable in the changed economic environment of the time.

Yet even after these additions, it was evident entering the 1998 lease negotiations that if the goal was to retain the team in western New York, additional revenue sources would be needed to keep the team economically viable compared to other much larger markets. While I was not a part of the formal lease discussions during this era, it is clear from an examination of the changes in the lease documents from the original twenty-five-year term to the 1998 lease extension that Erie County gave almost every revenue source it controlled to the team, and that the County further agreed to take on additional capital and operating costs.

It is important to understand the 1998 lease because the terms therein comprised a starting point for the lease negotiations of my administration. My team understood the Bills would not want to part with many of the concessions they received during the 1998 lease, and many other terms reached in 1998 would also continue from a practical standpoint (e.g., control of construction manager, choice of architects) during our discussions.

Additionally, when the 1998 lease agreement was finalized, a new partner entered the equation: New York State. During the first twenty-five-year lease term, Erie County leased the stadium directly to the Bills. Under the 1998 lease agreement, the County entered into a master lease agreement with the Erie County Stadium Corporation ("ECSC"), a not-for-profit public benefit corporation created by New York State, through its Empire State Development Division, to be the State's arm during the transaction, and then ECSC subleased the facility to the Bills.

Why was this done in the 1998 lease? Because New York State agreed to pay $63,250,000 for the cost of construction for a number of projects, including, but not limited to, the construction of six new club seating areas, all new dugout suites, and a new training facility. In order for the State to pay for the costs of construction, it had to have a legal interest in the stadium and adjoining facilities, and that legal interest was a "leasehold interest," in legal parlance. That is why New York State "leased" the stadium facility from the County and then subleased it to the football team.

However, the "cost" of the 1998 lease agreement to all public entities did not end there, especially as it pertained to Erie County's portion of expenses. New York State also agreed to provide the Bills $3 million annually for "working capital," and an additional $14,677,000 in other costs during the first year of the 1998 lease for construction overruns, additional rent to the Bills (yes, the State paid rent to the Bills for a stadium the Bills leased from the State), and additional rent costs to the County to make up for the County's cost in forfeiting revenue it expected to receive during the 1998 and 1999 budget years.

Additionally, Erie County agreed to make an annual capital payment to the Bills for costs associated with maintaining the stadium, which averaged $2.55 million per year, and totaled $38,291,000 during the fifteen-year life of the 1998 lease. The County's annual capital contribution went toward basic preventative maintenance costs, such as shoring up concrete work, as well as the purchase of large capital items, such as the new Mitsubishi scoreboard during the last years of the 1998 lease agreement.

The County also agreed to pay the Bills a capped amount annually for costs associated with the Bills' game-day and other operating expenses. The game-day and operating expenses could be used by the Bills for just about any expenses related to the operation of the facility during each lease year. This "game-day" expense increased annually, and averaged approximately $3.5 million per year for a combined fifteen-year total of $53,108,000 during the life of the lease.

In the end, the 1998 lease did not cost just $63 million, as was reported repeatedly by media sources, but $214,326,000: $122,927,000 from New York State and $91,399,000 from Erie County. The split of public funds was roughly 57 percent from the State and 43 percent from the County (this ratio calculation would come into play during the 2013 lease negotiations). The County also gave up the right to collect revenues from every stadium-related source it had before. So, the true cost to the County was even more than the $91,399,000 the County paid out. But what is difficult to quantify is how much the cost to the region would have been if the team moved to another city back in 1998. Economically, the impact of losing the team would not be the same as when Bethlehem Steel closed up its operations in my hometown of Lackawanna. However, the impact on the region's psyche would be substantial and a significant blow to the city's view nationwide.

Finally, the 1998 lease introduced a new concept to the parties: a buyout provision. Starting in the sixth year of the 1998 lease agreement (2004), the team could inform the County and the State by February 28 that it was invoking its right to buy out the remaining years of the lease by paying a "termination fee." The buyout provision was not a one-time only option; the Bills could invoke the provision in each year remaining in the lease. As each year passed, the termination fee was reduced significantly. During the first year of the buyout, the fee was $20 million. It was subsequently reduced by $3 million during the second and third years of the buyout, and by $2 million for each year thereafter. As a result, by the last year of the buyout (2012), the termination fee diminished to $2 million. In other words, for the cost of a backup linebacker, Mr. Wilson or a subsequent owner could have moved the team, and the community would have had no recourse.

All the cards lay in the hands of the Bills' owner. Mr. Wilson insisted he would never move the team while he was alive, nor would he ever sell the team. If he had passed away before the end of the 1998 lease's term, and the team was sold to an out-of-town owner, the team might have been moved simply through payment of the termination fee. No one could have stopped it. No specific performance provision required the team to stay during the final years. Thankfully, Mr. Wilson survived the 1998 lease and kept his promise to the city—he never moved the team—but as the 1998 lease neared expiration, the possibility of losing the Bills once again loomed heavy.

Chapter 2

Starting from Scratch

The future of the Bills in western New York became an issue in my race for county executive in 2011. Chris Collins was the incumbent county executive seeking a second term after having been elected in 2007. I was the incumbent county comptroller, the county's chief fiscal officer, having been first elected in 2005 at the height of a major fiscal crisis in the county, and then reelected in 2009. Not many political prognosticators gave me much of a chance against Collins at the beginning of my race. He held a significant financial advantage over me, especially considering he could self-fund his campaign, and I could not, and he was a first-term incumbent. No first-term incumbent county executive had ever been defeated seeking reelection.

While I went into the race knowing I could lose, I never believed my candidacy was a suicide mission. I did not run just to be a name on the ballot against the incumbent, as happens so often in politics. If I could get my message of responsible leadership out to the community, I knew I could win. I had already established a reputation for being the taxpayers' fiscal watchdog and successfully won two countywide campaigns. I knew I was not expected to win in most pundit circles, but I like being the underdog. When no one gives me a chance of succeeding, it only strengthens my resolve and efforts to prove the so-called experts wrong.

There were many issues central to the race—proper funding levels for libraries and cultural institutions, defining "essential" services to the public, the role of government, who the county executive works for and must answer to (short answer: the people), among many others—but one issue that rarely came up early on was the Bills lease. In February 2011, when asked by a local television reporter whether he had begun talks with the Bills regarding a new lease, Collins responded, "I've had preliminary discussions, absolutely."

At the time, I was not surprised to hear Collins say it. I assumed he had commenced discussions. If I were in his position, I would have done the same. He understood, as I did, that any county executive who wanted to continue his political career must complete a successful lease negotiation with the team. Or at least I thought he would have believed this fact; because after the interview in February 2011, any discussions about lease negotiations seem to disappear. This was good news for my campaign.

Throughout 2011, my campaign staff was certain Collins was secretly negotiating a deal with Mr. Wilson, Russ Brandon, the chief executive officer for the team, or Jeff Littmann, the chief financial officer for the Bills and the team's chief negotiator during the 1998 lease process. I did not expect a final lease to be formalized, but we all expected a deal would be revealed when it mattered the most politically—about one month before the general election.

These "October Surprise" events, as they are known in the political parlance, seem to happen all the time in major elections. No matter what happens during the campaign, expect something to happen during the last few weeks before the election that will alter, or at least impact, the final result. Furthermore, if you can control the release of a positive development for your candidacy, ideally by not releasing it until just before the general election is held, the better for you in the final outcome.

Having been the comptroller for a number of years, I was able to develop good relations with many County employees who worked in the departments controlled by the county executive, especially the long-time civil servants. I kept inquiring behind the scenes with these good sources, as well with individuals I knew in Governor Andrew M. Cuomo's office in New York State to find out what actually was happening between the parties to the negotiations. I kept getting the same reports back: nothing was happening. My staff members who inquired received the same message.

I found it hard to believe Collins was doing nothing. If I had been in his shoes as executive I certainly would have been doing all I could to wrap up a deal as soon as possible. My staff and I all believed that something must be going on, even if it was limited to very quiet negotiations between the Bills and the County, with no State involvement.

Then, in September 2011, *The Buffalo News* reported Collins was "waiting to hear from the Bills," and that "a study" was being performed by the team on the stadium's needs. I do not remember what hit the floor first, my jaw or the newspaper, but I was flabbergasted after reading the story. After months of being afraid to bring up the Bills lease on the campaign trail, assuming Collins would reap the advantage of it when he announced a new deal, immediately I realized the Bills lease would become a significant issue in the campaign, and one I could talk about without fear of repercussions.

On October 13, 2011, during our only televised debate of the campaign, I brought up the failure of Collins to properly negotiate a new lease. We knew from poll data that Collins had a reputation for being arrogant, and his "waiting" for the Bills to come to him fit perfectly into that narrative. Thus, when the opportunity arose, I criticized him for not being proactive and putting at risk the team becoming the "Los Angeles Bills" or the "Toronto Bills."

Collins's response to my critique also fit perfectly into this narrative. "Mr. Poloncarz knows nothing about what's going on in the negotiations," he said with some arrogance. "I see a successful conclusion to these negotiations."

While the discussion on the Bills lease was just one small part of the debate, it was emblematic. I kept throwing punches at him, requiring him to respond. Walking off the debate stage, I felt certain I had won. My staff was jubilant, and we knew Collins's staff was down just from their facial expressions. While there was no official spin room like at presidential or gubernatorial debates, reporters were present, and most of their questions played off shots I took at Collins.

In the days that followed, I knew I won the debate because I kept hearing the same response from the public—they could not believe Collins would be so arrogant as to wait for the Bills to come to him. I heard over and over the same basic refrain: "Doesn't he realize how important the Bills are to this community?"

In the debate, Collins said I knew nothing about the negotiations with the team. He was right—I did not. No matter how hard I had tried, I couldn't find out anything about the alleged negotiations. After the debate, I concluded there were no negotiations to know about; otherwise, Collins would have been much better prepared to respond to the questions about the lease by revealing something about these negotiations—dates of meetings, general status reports to the public, anything.

Mr. Wilson pretty much confirmed negotiations had not commenced when *The Buffalo News* published an article on October 30, 2011, quoting him as saying, "We just want a decent football stadium, and we'll take care of that when we talk to the State and the County." The key word in his response was "when." He did not say, "We have already talked to the County about a decent football stadium." He said, "*when* we talk."

Additionally, in response to a question about what protections the State and County were seeking, Mr. Wilson responded, "We haven't gotten anywhere near that." Both of these quotes, coming this late in the campaign, confirmed that serious negotiations had yet to take place. There would be no "October Surprise" in the election as it pertained to a new Bills lease, and to the degree a surprise existed, it benefitted me: the public now knew lease negotiations were nonexistent.

And the rest, as they say, is history. On November 8, 2011, I proved the political pundits and prognosticators wrong by defeating Chris Collins with a comfortable margin of 53 to 47 percent, thereby being elected Erie County's eighth county executive. The charge of securing a new lease with the Bills fell to me, and I was determined not to fumble this responsibility.

While I had heard nothing about lease discussions, I assumed the County's team had moved forth with *some* efforts to secure a lease, at least internally. I expected the County to have compiled plenty of analysis and reports, especially considering we owned the stadium, and I could rely on this data and information as I went forward. If anyone knew the condition of the stadium and what was needed to modernize it, surely it was the Erie County Department of Public Works.

I soon discovered the County had done nearly nothing. An occasional phone call between Collins and a Bills official may have occurred, but that was it. The Department of Public Works had not commissioned any internal studies on the physical state of Ralph Wilson Stadium. The county attorney's office had not retained outside counsel with experience in recent NFL lease transactions to assist it during the lease negotiations. The county's Environment and Planning Department has not been asked to assist in any lease-related activity.

While the team had retained the architectural and engineering firm Populous to do a needs study, the County had apparently done nothing—at least nothing that showed any evidence of progress. If something had been done, the materials had been destroyed. Based on many other documents turned over to us during the transition phase between our administrations, I discounted the destruction of materials as a plausibility. This left but one option: the prior administration had made no progress toward negotiating a new lease.

I was starting from scratch.

Chapter 3

The First Meeting

About a week after my victory, I discussed with Sam Hoyt, Regional President for the Empire State Development Corporation, the idea of setting up a "meet and greet" between the two of us and representatives of the Bills. I had known Sam for many years: he was my former representative in the New York State Assembly, we had worked together on many political races over the years (including on our own mutual races), and he had recently left the Assembly to be Governor Andrew M. Cuomo's point person in western New York for economic development. Sam indicated he was aware of no discussions involving New York State and the Bills, and with the upcoming change of County administrations, the time had arrived for the State to become involved.

I told Sam it would be better for me to meet before I was sworn in as executive because my schedule was already starting to fill up with meeting requests in the months of January and February 2012, and I wanted to get the ball moving on the matter as soon as possible. Sam agreed to set up the meeting since my staff and I were thigh-high in all matters related to the transition to my administration. Plus, if Sam set up the meeting, we could keep it more secretive. The longstanding rumor in county government is that the Rath Building's walls have ears, and in my ten-plus years as an elected official in Erie County government, nothing has happened to prove to me otherwise.

In short order the meeting was set for lunch on November 21, 2011, at the Buffalo Club. I indicated I would be attending the meeting alone because, at the time, I had yet to name any key cabinet appointees for my administration—the transition team had just begun sorting through resumes. Sam indicated he would be the sole representative of the State, and we would be meeting with either two or three team representatives. A few days before the meeting it was confirmed that Russ Brandon and Jeff Littmann would be representing the team.

In between scheduling the meeting and finding out who would attend, I received an invitation to attend a reception at the New York governor's mansion in Albany. The reception was for various officials from across the state who had won recent elections—a nice perk for those of us who had just come off grueling campaigns. For many officials, this reception might be the first, or only, time they would meet the governor. For me, I had met Governor Cuomo many times before, including holding joint press conferences with him when he was attorney general and I was comptroller. While I was honored to be invited, the thought of driving four and half hours from Buffalo to Albany for a two-hour reception was not very appealing. Regardless, I attended the reception because I wanted to talk to the governor about one key issue—getting a new Bills lease negotiated as soon as possible.

So, on November 16, a staff member and I left Buffalo around nine in the morning, drove to Albany, got in town just in time to meet with a few state officials at the capitol building, checked into our hotel afterward to freshen up, and got ready to attend the reception. Entry into the reception at the mansion was by invite only, with a few New York State police officers, in full trooper regalia, confirming everyone's entrance at the main gate and then at the front door once again. Upon entrance I recognized a number of elected officials from other parts of the state, talked to them, and then made a beeline to the governor, who was at the head of a long reception line waiting to meet him.

The governor was standing next to a fireplace with a picture of former President and Governor of New York Franklin D. Roosevelt above its mantle—an imposing sight. He was talking to each person for about thirty seconds and then posing for a picture. I was about to queue up in line when one of the governor's closest advisors, Joe Percoco, pulled me out of the line and took me directly up to see the governor. I reached out my hand. The governor instead gave me a big hug and congratulated me on my victory. I thanked him for his assistance in my race and told him I looked forward to working with him on many issues, with no issue being more important than keeping the Bills in Buffalo.

At that moment the governor stepped away from the fireplace, and we talked about the Bills for a few minutes, far longer than the thirty seconds everyone else was getting. While the governor knew the lease expired after the 2013 season, he was not aware of some of the other details at that point, including the fact that the Bills could still buy out the final year of the 1998 lease. I was not surprised he didn't know about the buyout option, as there had been no real conversations on the topic, and I doubted he had been advised of all the terms of the current lease. Additionally, I mentioned to him the upcoming meeting to be held and attended by Sam Hoyt, Bills officials, and myself. I was not sure if he even knew about the meeting before I told him about it.

The governor stated he knew how important it was to the people of western New York to keep the Bills in Buffalo, and he was deeply committed to getting a lease completed in due time. While he knew the lease was to expire prior to the 2013 season, he did not indicate to me a sense of urgency toward resolving the matter. He agreed to talk to me very soon about the current lease and said he looked forward to a report from Sam on the upcoming meeting.

I thanked the governor for his support of my candidacy, for his time, and for his commitment to the community. Then his photographer summoned us back to the fireplace, and we stood under the Roosevelt portrait and had our picture taken. Before leaving the mansion, I talked to a few more officials and guests. However, no matter what else I did that night, I knew I had accomplished what I had set out to do: getting the governor to focus on one of the most important issues he would have to address in western New York—a new lease for the Buffalo Bills.

With this meeting out of the way, I could now focus on the upcoming meeting with team officials. The Buffalo Club was chosen as the location for the meeting because (1) we could meet in a private room, and (2) it would not be strange to see any of the participants at the Club. While I am not a member of the Club, I have attended many breakfasts, lunches, and meetings there over the years, as have Sam, Russ, and Jeff. So if anyone happened to see any of us in the Club individually, they wouldn't have wondered why we were there.

Arriving a few minutes before the meeting was scheduled to begin, I was advised by the Club's front host of the location of the meeting room and that the Bills' "attendees" were already present. I thought to myself, "so much for secrecy." Then Sam walked in, and together we climbed the massive stairs that led to the second floor, the location of our meeting.

Walking into the room, I saw Russ at the end of the table on the far side from the door, while Jeff was sitting in the middle. We exchanged pleasantries, and I sat down next to Russ and across from Jeff, as Sam took the last seat immediately to my left and next to the door.

Though I had seen Russ interviewed on television by local media in the past, it was the first time I had met him in person. I was surprised to be taller than Russ, as I had judged from his interviews he was bigger. I have felt this reaction on the other end when I meet people who know me only from television. Usually they assume I am six foot two or greater, when in fact I am five eleven. Russ was dressed impeccably well, wearing cufflinks and a suit and shirt I could tell was out of my price range as county comptroller.

Russ was not a football player. From my limited knowledge before our meeting, I knew he had been a fairly accomplished baseball player at St. John Fisher College in Rochester. But he had realized early on that if he was going to make it to the majors it would not be as a player. He had worked his way up the ladder to an upper-management position with the Florida Marlins. If there was any doubt that the Marlins had won a World Series during Russ's tenure there, the large World Series Champions ring on his finger quickly answered the question.

Russ's reputation was as a marketing guru. He knew how to market any product, including a poorly performing sports franchise, and get the best return possible in sales. While the Bills had not performed too well on the field for many years, the team still sold out many home games and had recently moved one home regular-season game to Toronto each season to capitalize on the growing NFL market in southern Ontario.

Knowing Russ's background in marketing, I knew to be wary of taking his statements at face value. This is not to say I didn't trust Russ, but his day job entailed putting his best face forward and making lemonade out of lemons. I understood I had to parse the marketing from Russ's statements to get to the heart of the matter.

I knew Russ was approximately my age. In fact, we were both forty-four years old when the negotiations started. At the time, I thought to myself, "We're two fairly young guys from Generation X to have the future of the Buffalo Bills in our hands." I already knew that if I planned on having any future career in politics, I better not screw up the team's future in Buffalo.

Jeff Littmann was the chief financial officer for the Buffalo Bills, but I had been told by people who had met him that he was much more than that—he was Ralph Wilson's accountant, lawyer, advisor, and confidant for many years. I had heard that Ralph treated Jeff like a son, and Jeff treated Ralph like a second father. I was also told to expect him to be all business.

Jeff was exactly as I expected: a no-nonsense man who exuded all-seriousness. He reminded me of successful clients I had represented while practicing law at Kavinoky Cook, LLP: a businessman who achieved success by making smart, calculated decisions and not being afraid to walk away from a deal when it was not in his best interest, even if it meant leaving scorched earth behind for others to clean up. I quickly realized that every word Jeff uttered counted. There would be no mistaken revelations during these negotiations. Suffice to say, Jeff is not a man for extraneous small talk.

I was thus determined to listen intently to every word Jeff stated, and to read any correspondence from him with a fine-tooth comb. Jeff reminded me of the late Arnold Gardner, one of my legal mentors at Kavinoky Cook. Arnold taught me the value of using just the right word in a sentence—that every word and punctuation mark has a purpose. Having represented men and women like Jeff in the past, and having dealt with Arnold Gardner's red pen rewrite treatment at Kavinoky Cook, I knew careful attention should be devoted to Jeff's words, including trying to glean a secret meaning from his statements.

We ordered lunch, and as the waiter took the others' orders, I observed the room more closely. The meeting room at the Buffalo Club is just as you would expect in the preeminent club in downtown Buffalo: high ceilings, walls paneled in ornate dark wood, and a table in the center that could sit six at most, four comfortably. I wondered what the walls of this room might reveal if they could talk.

When I had left for the Club, I deliberately left my notepad behind. I wanted to look like I was unprepared. I wanted the Bills' representatives to think I was a lightweight. I wanted them to underestimate me. As I said earlier, I feel I perform best when others underestimate me. However, while I might have looked unprepared, I knew from attending previous meetings at the Buffalo Club that a pen and pad of paper bearing the Club's logo would be next to every place setting. So I left my portfolio behind, and when I walked into the room the pad of paper and pen were there.

After ordering lunch, Sam commenced the discussion. He noted how it was "a top priority" of the Cuomo administration to get a long-term lease done and that the State would be an active participant again, as it had been in 1998. Sam noted he had spoken to the governor about this topic and the governor was committed to getting a long-term deal done, and that was about the extent of Sam's participation in the meeting. After his brief opening, I do not remember Sam saying much more other than asking a few questions of Russ and Jeff.

Russ then began the conversation from the Bills' perspective. He discussed the difficulties of marketing an NFL team in a small market, and how successful the "Toronto experiment" had been. He noted how the team had changed its marketing focus from the Buffalo and western New York region to Rochester and areas eastward in upstate New York and northward to Toronto. He said it made no sense to go west past the New York state line because Erie, Pennsylvania, was split pretty evenly between Cleveland Browns and Pittsburgh Steelers fans. So if the Bills were looking to grow their market, they had two choices: upstate New York or the more lucrative and larger Toronto market.

Russ explained how, in 2007, the Bills had entered into a five-year agreement with Rogers Media in Southern Ontario in which, starting in 2008, Rogers "purchased" one regular and one preseason home game from the Bills and moved the games to the Rogers Centre in Toronto. Russ noted that the Bills made approximately twice as much by selling a home game to Rogers Communications than if they held the same game at Ralph Wilson Stadium—guaranteed income for the team even if not a single ticket had been sold for the game by Rogers.

As county comptroller at the time, I knew the team needed approval from Erie County to hold any home game outside of Ralph Wilson Stadium, as doing so technically violated terms of the 1998 lease agreement. Former County Executive Joel Giambra granted such authority in 2007, meaning the five-year agreement with Rogers and the County's acquiescence to it would expire at the same time as the current lease agreement.

Russ noted how important the Canadian market had become to the team. He stated Canadians made up nearly 20 percent of the attendees at games at Ralph Wilson Stadium and that this percentage of ticket buyers increased substantially from the years prior to the Rogers deal. He noted how the organization wanted to continue the arrangement with Rogers and how Rogers wanted to do the same.

In this discussion, Russ also used for the first time the word that in my mind would highlight his marketing background: "inventory." Instead of describing the people in the seats at a home game at Ralph Wilson Stadium as our fans, he described them as "inventory sold." This is not to say Russ did not talk about the fan experience or the team's fans in general, but when it came to selling seats for games, fans were strictly inventory in his eyes.

Hearing this was jarring at first, but in the end it helped me to understand the team's goals in reaching an equitable lease agreement. It might have been the first time I really viewed the franchise as being anything other than the team on the field. It was also a business selling its inventory to the general public, and that was something I needed to understand as the lease negotiation process moved forward.

Russ went on to note that "without the Canadian market it is doubtful the Bills could remain economically competitive with other teams in the league." I assumed this to be true, but at this point Jeff interrupted Russ to clarify his statement. This interruption was my first indication that though Russ was the chief executive officer of the Bills and Jeff the chief financial officer, Jeff was going to be in charge of the lease negotiations.

Jeff interrupted Russ to note Mr. Wilson's expectation was not to be in a comparable class with the highest revenue-generating teams in the league but to be in the "middle market territory." Jeff then took over the discussion. He gave an overview of the prior lease deals, including the investments made by the team through the years, and then began to give a tutorial comparing the current collective bargaining agreement between the owners and the players' association to the prior one.

Jeff noted that under the prior collective bargaining agreement, the Bills were in the "lowest quartile of teams" in regards to annual revenue. This was an example of Jeff choosing exactly the word he wanted to use, as I had not heard anyone use the word "quartile" in many, many years, or maybe ever. Most people would say we are in the lowest "quarter" or "twenty-five percent," but Jeff used "quartile," and he would always use that word going forward during our discussions in regards to the Bills' annual revenues compared to other NFL teams' revenues.

Jeff remarked that if the prior collective bargaining agreement were still in place, we would be having a completely different discussion, but it was not. He said the current collective bargaining agreement "was fair, but with its challenges." He noted that under the current agreement, the Bills could realistically be in the "middle market territory" as it pertained to revenue. The current agreement generally ensured the Bills would be in at least the third, and maybe the lower end of the second quartile. Assuming market conditions did not change much from the current collective bargaining agreement and lease, the Bills could be financially successful in Buffalo.

I asked Jeff a number of questions regarding the terms of the current collective bargaining agreement and what teams he believed the Bills were comparable to on the balance sheet. He noted, and Russ confirmed, that it would be hard to say exactly because many of the determining factors regarding revenue generation and expenses are kept secret by each team. While each team is required to provide the league full information on all aspects of shared revenue, other revenue streams need not be revealed.

Jeff stated that the amount of advertising revenue a team receives from national or local businesses was an area in which the Bills could *not* compete with other markets. He stated the Bills could never match the amount of revenue received by teams in major markets, and we were even behind the eight-ball compared to other small- to mid-market communities.

Russ then noted the example of how the Bills received nothing, or next to nothing, from *The Buffalo News* in advertising revenue. This was a serious bone of contention for the team because *The Buffalo News* generated millions of dollars in sales as a result of its Bills coverage, and nothing was provided back to the team in revenue from the paper. According to Russ, in most other cities, the local newspaper would pay the team a substantial fee annually to be known as the "official newspaper" or "official media outlet" for the local team, or at least buy advertising space inside the stadium. But in Buffalo this was not the case. It became quite clear to me that the Bills did not hold *The Buffalo News* in high regard.

Sam and I asked for Jeff's and Russ's thoughts on where the next collective bargaining agreement would go. Both said it was too early to tell because the agreement did not expire until after the 2020 season. Jeff did note that if the next agreement was similar to the current one he saw no reason why the team could not continue to be successful in Buffalo, but a return to the terms of the prior agreement would not be welcome news at One Bills Drive. Russ concurred with his opinion.

I did not know the specifics of the terms of the current collective bargaining agreement, nor the prior one. However, I did remember Mr. Wilson decried the prior agreement as one pitting the large markets against the smaller market franchises, and that the smaller market franchises were coming out on the losing end. When the new agreement was entered into, Mr. Wilson noted it was a much better agreement for markets like Buffalo's and ensured smaller markets could compete for players and revenue with larger markets. So while I did not know all the details about the collective bargaining agreement, I was not surprised to hear Jeff and Russ conclude the team could be successful in the future if the current collective bargaining agreement's terms continued.

Jeff then noted the Bills had retained Populous to examine the condition of Ralph Wilson Stadium and generate ideas for major changes to make the stadium more economically viable. He did not expect the report to be ready until sometime during the first quarter (not quartile) of 2012. I asked if the Bills intended to share the full Populous report and corresponding schematics with the County and State, and Jeff said they would. In fact, Jeff said they would share all "factual information" related to the designs, which I would have expected because the stadium is owned by the County and we would need to have ownership of all architectural drawings of the facility.

Finally, I asked Jeff and Russ if the team had any interest in a new stadium or if they were satisfied with the Ralph continuing to be the home of the Bills. Having read reports in which Mr. Wilson noted he was not interested in a "Taj Mahal," but instead wanted "a decent football stadium," I assumed the answer would be no to the first question and yes to the second. Russ responded as I assumed, noting that at this time the stadium, with certain significant changes, would suffice for the immediate future.

Russ and Jeff wrapped up their presentation, and it was now my turn. I thanked them for their time, for Mr. Wilson's commitment to the region, and for agreeing to share all information as we moved forward. I noted I was presently heavily involved in choosing my cabinet, and while there were a few things I would wait to discuss with the parties until that process was complete, there was a key term the County would be seeking: the lease had to include a non-relocation agreement tied to the full length of the lease's term.

I did not express to those present my displeasure with the then current lease agreement, which included a buyout clause that could be effectuated annually by the team starting in year six of the lease. While the 1998 lease's term was for fifteen years, the team could buy out any year starting in year six by paying a termination fee that started at $20 million and declined significantly in each subsequent year. My goal was to ensure I could get the longest term possible with every year of the lease guaranteed, or at least avoid the declining buyout provision as contained in the then current lease.

I stated I was expecting a lease term of at least fifteen years. I knew the length would depend on the amount of investment from the government sector, but at the time I did not disclose that fact. I also knew that if the stadium's condition was as good as I'd been told, a twenty-year lease was not out of the realm of possibility, if the State and County invested hundreds of millions of dollars. If the investment was less, a fifteen-year agreement could still be expected, following the basic terms of the then current agreement. So I expressed my belief that only a very long-term agreement would be acceptable.

Jeff responded that all issues were open for negotiation, but the length and non-relocation agreement for the entire term would depend on the totality of governmental investment, as I figured the team would respond. He noted a similar annual buyout provision during the final years of the next lease would be what the team would expect, but everything would be negotiable.

I then spoke of my understanding that the stadium was generally in good shape from a structural standpoint, and asked whether the expectation from the team was that any renovations would be of a structural nature or related to generating more income from new luxury boxes and the like. Russ noted that the physical viability of the stadium and economic viability were not one and the same. He said he did not think new luxury boxes would be necessary, but certain changes would be required to keep the team economically viable.

I then asked the one question of Jeff and Russ I needed to ask and hoped would be answered in the negative: did the Bills intend on exercising the buyout provision for the final year of the 1998 lease? The Bills could have provided notice to the County and the State by February 28, 2012, of their intention to buy out the final year of the lease for $2 million. I assumed the answer would be no, as it would be silly to hold a meeting on future lease negotiations if the Bills intended to exercise the final buyout option. Yet, I was worried the team might exercise the option in order to put pressure on the County and State and negotiate from a position of strength.

Jeff gave me his word the team would not exercise its option to terminate the 1998 lease prior to the expiration of its full term. He said Mr. Wilson had no intention of moving the team during his lifetime. He assured me I would not receive any correspondence by February 28, 2012, informing me of the team's intention to terminate. I thanked him for his straightforward answer and his assurance and asked him to please pass on to Mr. Wilson my thanks for his commitment to Buffalo.

With that, after about ninety minutes of discussions, we agreed the first meeting was productive. We exchanged contact information, agreed to not set up the next meeting until sometime in February or March of 2012, and then shook hands and went our separate ways. I remember walking out of the Buffalo Club thinking, "I need to have the right team working for me if I am going to get a good lease agreement for the community." In my eyes, the only good agreement would be one that bound the team to the community for many years to come.

Chapter 4

Finding the Right Team

Following my election as county executive, I immediately got to work on filling key appointments in my administration. Erie County government is a large organization. There are more than four thousand employees and, as executive, I prepare and manage a budget of approximately $1.7 billion. To manage such an entity, I would need many qualified, experienced staff members at my side, including nearly thirty department heads. To accomplish the task of finding these individuals, I employed a volunteer transition team.

The transition team was headed by local real estate developer Michael Joseph and made up of an executive committee of Michael and thirteen other members, and six subcommittees comprising executive committee members and another fifty-two volunteers. These individuals were tasked with sifting through the hundreds of résumés we were receiving, eliminating those who did not meet the qualification requirements, interviewing others, and making recommendations to me. However, there was one position I wanted to fill myself without help from others: deputy county executive.

Early in my campaign, I had stated my deputy county executive would not be employed as a chief operating officer, as Mr. Collins had done, but as my economic development "czar." I wanted an individual experienced in the nuances of economic development, someone who knew the history of economic development in Erie County, both the successes and the many failures, and what would be required to move the community forward. While I had my own vision of and plans for economic development, and I expected my deputy to initiate many of these plans, I needed a person in this position who commanded the respect of the local business and economic development community and who would instantly show the world I meant business when I said I was hiring an economic development czar.

While discussing the issues with a number of people, I kept hearing the same refrain: "You need a Rich Tobe type of person as your deputy." After hearing this from the fourth or fifth individual I said to myself, "I don't need a Rich Tobe type of person—I need Rich Tobe."

Richard M. Tobe's history in government goes back decades. He has been a key advisor and counsel to Assemblyman William B. Hoyt, counsel to various New York State Assembly committees, former Commissioner of Environment and Planning in Erie County during the Gorski administration, counsel to various other officials, and Economic Development Head during Buffalo Mayor Byron Brown's first few years in office. During recent years, Rich had been independently consulting for a number of state governments on economic development issues, but he still lived in Buffalo.

I had met Rich on a few occasions before my election but considered him nothing more than an acquaintance. I had not dealt with him on an issue either in my career as an attorney or as county comptroller. Not knowing Rich well, I asked a friend who knew him to ask him if the job of deputy county executive piqued his interest at all. I heard back that it did. Based on that conversation, I called Rich to discuss my view of economic development and the issues I would face going forward as executive, including negotiating a new Bills lease. We had a cordial conversation and agreed to meet at his house.

On December 2, 2011, I walked up to a stately colonial house in one of Buffalo's nicest neighborhoods and was met at the door by Rich and his wife, Susan. Rich came prepared with a number of documents for me to review regarding methods of economic development. We had a very good conversation on a number of topics for approximately two hours. Included in the conversation was a discussion about the upcoming lease negotiations.

I informed Rich I had met with Jeff, Russ, and Sam on November 21, and that very little had occurred otherwise. I remember Rich asking had the County retained outside counsel to represent it during the negotiations. I said it had not, and he looked irritated. His irritation was not directed to me but toward the previous administration for failing to get the ball rolling. It indicated to him the lack of effort put in by the prior administration and, based on his own experience in negotiating the 1998 lease, how far behind the County actually was.

I asked Rich a number of questions about the prior lease and for his impressions of Jeff and Russ. He gave me a brief overview of the events that led to the 1998 lease and what he viewed as essential terms for the Bills going forward.

Rich stated he did not know Russ but that he knew Jeff very well. He noted if Jeff agreed to a provision, it meant Mr. Wilson agreed to the provision, and a "handshake deal" was all one needed to know the terms would be adhered to by the Bills. While every term would eventually be put into a final document, once you had the word of Jeff, meaning Mr. Wilson, you could be guaranteed the team would not try to alter the term. In Mr. Wilson's world, a handshake between parties was enough to seal the deal. Knowing this, I felt relieved to know the Bills would keep their word and not buy out the final year of the 1998 lease. Jeff had told me they would not do so, and he would prove true to his word.

During our conversation, it became clear to me that Rich's view of economic development meshed quite nicely with mine and that his knowledge from the previous lease negotiations would be invaluable to my administration. We exchanged goodbyes and, after I spoke to a few individuals whom I greatly respected regarding their views of Rich (all of which were positive), I offered him the position of deputy county executive. Thankfully, for me and especially for the community, he accepted the offer.

On December 12, 2011, at a press conference in the county comptroller's conference room, I officially introduced Rich as my deputy county executive. I spoke of Rich's long history in economic development, how he would be tasked with leading my administration's efforts to spur our local economy, and how he would be a key part of my team negotiating the new Bills lease.

I knew I made the right decision for this important position when, on December 14, 2011, *The Buffalo News'* lead editorial was entitled, "the right man for the job." The editorial went on to praise my selection of Rich, noting that "Tobe was at the forefront of lease negotiations for the Gorski administration in 1998, the last time the Bills and Erie County worked out a stadium lease, and that institutional knowledge should serve Poloncarz and taxpayers." With this important position settled, and having received glowing support of the choice from *The Buffalo News*, I could now focus on hiring other personnel for my administration.

While I eventually interviewed many individuals for key leadership positions throughout my administration—commissioners of health, senior services, environment and planning, and so on—two other department heads would be directly involved in Bills lease negotiations: the county attorney and the commissioner of the department of public works. I knew it was extremely important that I picked the right people for these positions.

The county attorney represents all county-elected officials, not just the county executive, including the sheriff, district attorney, clerk, comptroller, and legislators. In my view, I needed to appoint someone well respected in the legal community who could navigate the myriad potential conflicts that arise when elected officials do not see eye to eye.

Early in the process, I felt comfortable with Michael Siragusa as the incoming county attorney. Mike was the second assistant in charge of the New York State Attorney General's Buffalo office. I had known Mike for many years. The first time I met him we were on opposite sides of a federal court prisoner's civil rights case to which I had been assigned by U.S. District Court Judge John Curtin. Mike knew the intricacies and difficulties that can arise in representing a governmental entity, and had a reputation for being a fair litigator.

And it was a litigator I wanted as head of the county attorney's office. While I had practiced in many areas of the law as an attorney, I spent the majority of my career doing transactional work, such as closing the purchase and sale of businesses or the negotiation of complex real estate and finance transactions, and so did Rich Tobe. Thus, I wanted as the county's chief attorney a lawyer who had spent the vast majority of his or her career as a litigator. While I had a number of worthy candidates to choose from, Mike was my top choice.

My choice for commissioner of the department of public works (DPW) did not come so easily. My transition team would normally recommend four or five potential candidates for me to consider when filling a position. When it came to the commissioner of DPW, my transition team had only two recommendations.

I knew I had to choose the right person for commissioner of DPW because this individual would deal directly with the Bills lease. Because the County owns Ralph Wilson Stadium, it is responsible for its upkeep on an annual basis. Any lease negotiations would inevitably entail major structural changes to the stadium, and the commissioner of DPW would oversee that work.

I interviewed the two recommended candidates, and immediately disqualified one of them because the individual interviewed so poorly. The other candidate interviewed well, had the right experience, and seemed perfect for the position. I thought I had found my commissioner of DPW. I made the offer in late December 2011.

During the interview, and again when I made the offer, the individual noted that the only potential problem in accepting the job was the individual's partnership interest at a local engineering firm. In short, would the firm allow the candidate to leave without incurring a substantial financial penalty due to the firm's rules for early partnership withdrawal? By this time, I had started to publicly name a number of my appointees. I was getting many questions from inside and outside county government as to who my DPW commissioner would be.

I soon found myself in a bind when the candidate to whom I offered the position had to refuse because of the partnership with the engineering firm. It was getting very close to January 1 (my inauguration day), and snow was flying in Erie County—of course, the commissioner of DPW oversees road repair and snow removal. But I had no commissioner of DPW, and no alternative candidate looming. Or so I thought.

One person I had not considered for commissioner of DPW, but had immediately considered for the transition team's Public Works Subcommittee, was John Loffredo. John was the retired DPW commissioner, having served in that capacity for many years, first in the Dennis Gorski administration and then in the Joel Giambra administration. John was one of those rare survivors who moved himself up the ranks in the City of Buffalo and then Erie County, and who worked for both Democratic and Republican elected officials without being deemed political.

I first got to know John during my first two years as county comptroller. I found him to be personable and exceptionally knowledgeable. Though I did not get along with every member of the Giambra administration, I got along amicably with John. When he retired as commissioner of DPW at the end of the Giambra administration I wished him well, assuming his career as a public servant was over and that a well-deserved retirement awaited him.

When we were faced with no real option for commissioner of DPW, Tim Callan, the executive director of my transition team and soon-to-be deputy director of the Erie County Division of Budget and Management, suggested we should consider bringing John Loffredo out of retirement, at least for the first year. Tim previously worked for me as my associate deputy comptroller; before that, he worked for the Erie County Legislature as its primary budget analyst. Tim knew John from those times and had worked with him during the transition phase.

Tim generally did not recommend hiring an individual from a prior administration, as he thought we should make our own mark. He certainly felt we should not hire anyone from the Collins or Giambra administrations. However, Tim respected John and told me his qualifications were far superior to anyone who had applied for the position, which was not surprising since John had previously served as commissioner. Tim advised me to offer the position to John.

I asked Tim to reach out to John to see if he would be interested in serving in the position, even if only for a short time. Tim reported back to me that John was indeed interested in serving as commissioner again but that he had a stipulation related to the Bills, and John wanted to talk to me about it. So I called John and set up a meeting.

We met, discussed how his retirement was going, and I then asked him directly if he really wanted to come back and serve as commissioner again. John said he would be honored to return, but with one stipulation—he would serve only if he could do so through the entire duration of work at the stadium that would inevitably result following a new Bills lease. John noted how he had played a role in previous construction projects at the stadium, was a key member of County Executive Gorski's team during the 1998 lease negotiations and resulting construction therefrom, had spent many years at the stadium, knew it like the back of his hand, and he would consider it a crowning achievement of his career to be involved in what might be the final renovation project at the stadium.

I was shocked John would commit to serving for so long, as we both discussed how the construction at the stadium could theoretically go on through my entire first term. He said he had no interest in being a caretaker, and the thought of working on the stadium again excited him. I was thrilled to have as my commissioner an individual who was not only well respected and experienced, but who knew the Ralph like the back of his hand and who could immediately contribute to our efforts to secure a new lease. I told John if he accepted he could serve as long as he liked, certainly through the negotiations and construction phase of a new lease. He shook my hand, and like that I had my commissioner of DPW.

There were other commissioners and department heads I would hire who would play some role in the lease negotiations and construction work at the stadium: Maria Whyte, commissioner of the Department of Environment and Planning (and now my deputy county executive); Jesse Burnette, director of the Office of Equal Employment Opportunity; Dan Neaverth, Jr., commissioner of Emergency Services; Robert Keating, director of the Division of Budget and Management; and Frank Cammarata, director of the Office of the Disabled, to name a few. However, Rich Tobe, Mike Siragusa, John Loffredo, and myself, as well as our senior staffs, would play the key roles going forward for the County during the negotiations. Yet there remained one major piece of the puzzle to find before the County's team was complete: we needed to hire outside legal counsel to help represent the County.

While the entire Erie County Attorney's Office would be at my disposal during the lease negotiations to advise our team, it was essential that we also obtain legal counsel from the private sector. This outside counsel should have not only significant legal expertise on issues related to complicated transactions, but also specialized knowledge related to recent NFL stadium transactions.

I understood if the County was to be ready to move forward with negotiations when the Populous report was completed by the end of the first quarter of 2012, Mike Siragusa and I had to choose the County's outside legal counsel within the first ninety days of my term. To do so would require us to issue a request for proposals for firms to provide services to the County as soon as I became county executive. That is exactly what we did.

A request for proposals (RFP) is a device used by governments to get responses from parties interested in working on behalf of the government. An RFP will usually state the services required, cite the necessary qualifications required for a respondent, ask respondents to prove their qualifications in writing, and require respondents to specify how much they would charge for services rendered. While the county attorney has the power to hire outside counsel for any matter without issuing an RFP, I felt it necessary to open up the process to potential counsel nationwide so we could choose from a wealth of qualified firms.

So, on Tuesday, January 3, 2012, my first business day in office (I was sworn in on January 1, a Sunday, and Monday was a legal holiday), I issued my first executive order directing the county attorney's office to issue an RFP seeking outside counsel to assist the County in negotiating a new Bills lease. I actually issued five executive orders on a number of varying topics during my first official work day. However, to show the community how important it was to me to successfully negotiate a new Bills lease, the first executive order I issued was for the outside counsel RFP.

Sitting at my desk, with members of the local media surrounding me, I signed all the orders. The order pertaining to the Bills was the only order the media asked about. This would be a recurring theme throughout my tenure as executive: no matter how innocuous the subject matter might be, as long as it was about the Bills, the media demanded to know about it, disregarding anything else that might be happening in county government. Regardless, I signed the order, answered questions from the media, and showed off Rich Tobe's copy of the four-inch-thick book that comprised the 1998 lease agreement.

As a result of the order, on January 23, 2012, the county attorney's office issued a "Request for Proposal to Provide Legal Services in Connection with the Lease of the County's Professional Football Stadium" (the "Bills RFP"). The Bills RFP required all proposals to be returned to the county attorney's office by 3 p.m. on February 10, 2012, and noted the selection would be made by February 24, 2012. The Bills RFP required all respondents to include the following information: (1) "the firm's history and experience with providing legal services related to lease of professional or amateur sports facilities, real estate transactions and complex contractual matters . . . ;" (2) personnel who would be assigned to the services; (3) three clients the County could contact to discuss the firm's references; (4) any potential conflict of interests; and (5) a cost proposal, including all out-of-pocket expenses.

I expected to receive responses from many law firms in Buffalo, as well as others from elsewhere in the nation, and I was not disappointed by the number of respondents. In fact, fourteen responses were received by the deadline, with one law firm, Buffalo-based Phillips Lytle, withdrawing its response due to an undisclosed conflict of interest. Seven of the firms were either based in Buffalo or had a significant office in Buffalo; the other six were based in Houston, Cleveland, Atlanta, and other locations.

Most of the proposals were substantial in nature, though others looked as if they were put together at the last minute. Considering that being chosen to assist the County in closing the Bills lease would be considered a feather in the cap of any firm, I was surprised that some firms sent in such weak responses. My former legal mentors would have fired me if I had submitted a response so deficient in substance and appearance.

While the county attorney has complete discretion to retain the firm of his choice, Mike Siragusa employed an informal advisory review committee to review the responses, meet with some of the respondents, and advise him of their views of the respondents. The review committee included Rich Tobe, First Assistant County Attorney Michelle Parker, and myself. The advisory review committee and Mike Siragusa met with a number of the respondents before making a decision. These meetings were important because they gave us an opportunity to question the representatives of the firm and, even more so, because they revealed the personalities of the attorneys. For example, one out-of-state attorney with great credentials was unbelievably pompous, acting as though we were clueless clods who had no idea what we were doing and needed to choose him to successfully close the transaction. His arrogance disqualified him and his firm.

When properly prepared, law firms can shine during such meetings, and that is exactly what Nixon Peabody LLP did during the interview. While Nixon Peabody's main office is in New York City, it has had an office in Buffalo for many years. Mike Siragusa and I did not want to limit our choice to solely Buffalo firms, but extra points were given to firms with Buffalo offices. Nixon Peabody was represented by Chris Melvin, Martha Anderson, and Elizabeth Columbo. These attorneys previously represented the State of New Jersey in negotiations with the New York Jets and Giants for the Meadowlands, as well as the City of Indianapolis in negotiations that resulted in the construction of Lucas Oil Stadium. Additionally, Nixon Peabody represented New York State's Empire State Development Corporation during the 1998 Bills lease negotiations. So these attorneys were very experienced in complex sports lease transactions, as well as in the prior 1998 Bills lease.

Nixon Peabody also presented themselves as competent counsel—without overdoing it. They recognized that we knew what we were doing and acknowledged any counsel we chose would likely represent the County well. Chris Melvin was modest. He answered all our questions on point, without acting as if he was the only person who knew what he was doing. Martha Anderson, based in Buffalo, did the same.

Walking out of the meeting with Nixon Peabody, everyone felt comfortable with the principal partners of the firm, especially Mike Siragusa and Rich Tobe. This was an example of modesty combined with excellent credentials being chosen over well-credentialed arrogance. Just like when people pick an attorney to represent them during a house sale or in drafting a will, we knew we had to feel comfortable with the outside counsel the County chose because we would be working with these individuals for some time.

While we originally hoped to announce the County's choice of a firm by February 24, 2012, due to a number of factors, the decision was delayed until early March. So, after confirming in writing the rate per hour to be charged (a rate we agreed would not be disclosed per hour, though the aggregate amount paid would be disclosed under any Freedom of Information Law request), on March 9, 2012, we announced the County had retained Nixon Peabody LLP to assist the County during the Bills lease negotiations. With that, all the pieces of my team—the right team—were in place, and it was none too soon because lease negotiations had already started in earnest.

Chapter 5

Viability = D × P³ − C

During the end of the first month of my administration, Jeff Littmann contacted Rich Tobe to inform him that the Populous report was nearing completion and the parties should sit down for the first time. While the County had yet to choose its outside counsel, to move the process along we decided to meet as soon as a mutual date could be arranged by the parties. In short order, we agreed to meet on February 16, 2012, at my office's conference room on the sixteenth floor of the Rath Building.

Prior to the meeting, Rich Tobe and I discussed what, if anything, the County would reveal at this meeting. We agreed to let the Bills make their presentation and ask questions as necessary, but not to divulge any major position of the County at this time. The Bills wanted to meet and present their case, so to speak, so we decided to let them do so, and we would eventually respond. As part of our discussion, Rich dropped on my desk his copy of the 1998 lease agreement and said, "You might want to brush up on the agreements and basic terms contained in this."

While the idea of reading through a thousand-page-plus book containing multiple agreements did not appeal to me, I knew I had to do it to adequately prepare for the upcoming negotiations. So I spent the better part of a week reading through the Master Lease, Stadium Lease, Construction Coordinating Agreement, and other documents that comprised the 1998 lease transaction, occasionally asking Rich why such an action was taken.

It was during these prenegotiation discussions with Rich that I truly realized hiring him was really going to bear fruit during the upcoming lease talks. I already knew I had made a good decision in retaining him, but I *really* knew it during these talks. Rich has an encyclopedic memory. Several times while answering my questions, he related to me a phone conference or other discussion he had had with Jeff Littmann nearly fifteen years earlier. I knew by the time this first meeting was to be held the County would be prepared to make it a productive one.

So at 1 p.m. on February 16, 2012, I welcomed representatives of the Bills and New York State to the Rath Building. Representing the County were Rich Tobe, County Attorney Mike Siragusa, DPW Commissioner John Loffredo, and myself. The Bills were represented by Jeff Littmann, Russ Brandon, Mary Owen, and attorney Michael Schiavone from the law firm Lipsitz, Green, and Cambria. The State was represented by Sam Hoyt and Stephen Gawlik, counsel to the Empire State Development Corporation in Buffalo.

We had prepared an agenda to hand out to the parties, but we never distributed it because immediately after we exchanged pleasantries Jeff Littmann began to speak on what the team wanted in exchange for a new lease. At the same time, Russ handed out a confidential eight-page report the Bills' negotiating team wished to go over but which they asked be returned to them prior to the meeting's end. As will be discussed, in addition to information about the stadium, the report included demographic data regarding season and game-day ticket holders and total state payroll tax for the team's New York employees, information the team did not want subject to a Freedom of Information Law request at the time.

Jeff opened up by stating the team "doesn't want a new stadium" and they were not interested in a "complete rehab like Green Bay or Kansas City." He noted they were willing to sign a ten- to fifteen-year lease depending on the construction and operating expenses to be assumed by the State and County. Though I was a little surprised when he said the team was not interested in a major retrofit of the stadium, as had occurred at Green Bay or Kansas City, I was relieved to hear it because this meant the price tag for the work would be much less than it could have been.

He noted the team wanted to manage the construction process, but it would also assume the construction risks associated with the project, including paying for cost overruns. The team also wanted to choose the construction managers, engineers, and architects. Rich and I had already discussed these terms, which were similar to the prior lease, and they did not cause much consternation to us since professional services can be chosen by a noncompetitive procurement process under County and State law.

Jeff said the construction contractors would be chosen by the County pursuant to a competitive RFP process, which we assumed would happen because County and State law requires such a process for a County-owned project. Rich noted this follows the basic foundation used in the 1998 lease and was generally acceptable to the County with one caveat—that no one term could be deemed accepted by the parties until all terms were deemed acceptable. Rich and Jeff had already conversed about this subject matter and had agreed to the basic premise that any one agreed-upon term could be reviewed at a later date if another term changed the economics or substance of the total transaction. So, when Jeff said that was acceptable to the Bills, and Steve Gawlik said the same for the State, we had our first agreement among parties—no one term could be deemed agreed upon until all terms had been agreed upon. While it might not mean much toward the terms contained in the final agreement, at least it was a start.

Jeff then went over the eight-page presentation. He started by noting that all parties had kept their promises under the 1998 lease agreement, especially Mr. Wilson, who promised to keep the team in Buffalo during his life. While changes had been made based on the Toronto series, the basic terms of the lease had been met by all, which helped pave the way for the current negotiations.

Jeff then reviewed the condition of the stadium, noting it was generally good but that based on the team's estimate the stadium required at least $20 to $25 million of preventative maintenance. Speaking to Commissioner Loffredo after the meeting, he believed this estimate was a little high but not out of the realm of possibility depending on the work to be done. Jeff spent little time discussing the preventative maintenance required, instead turning his attention to the issue of operating expenses. He specifically noted game-day expenses had risen dramatically since the 1998 lease was signed, primarily in the areas of insurance coverage and energy—the events of September 11, 2001, had resulted in dramatically increased insurance premiums for the team, as well as increased energy expenses to run the entire complex.

None of this surprised me much. While the County is a self-insured entity and, except in very rare occasions, does not have insurance, we knew for some time the Bills' insurance expenses had increased greatly following the September 11 attacks. We also knew energy expenses had increased significantly, since our own energy bills, like everyone else's, had risen since 2001.

On page four of the report, the team claimed that between 1998 and the beginning of 2013 the team's actual operating and game-day expenses equaled $104,401,424, while the State and County "only" reimbursed the Bills for $54,199,854, resulting in the Bills absorbing $54,201,570 of expenses. (Though the team collected all copies of the report at the end of the meeting, I wrote down these figures in my notes during the meeting.) Jeff noted the unreimbursed percentage of expenses had grown significantly after the 2001 season and was impacting the team's net profits.

However, Jeff then stated that while these game-day and operating costs had increased significantly, the team "did not have to tap into the supplemental revenue pool" created by the NFL as a result of the most recent collective bargaining agreement. This was a clue as to the current economic state of the team—if the team did not need to tap into the supplemental revenue pool created for ailing teams, it meant the team was generally doing well. While I retained my assumption that Jeff would never say anything unless he had a purpose behind it, it seemed he might have unintentionally tipped his hand by telling us in this way that the team was making money, and probably lots of it.

Jeff's next statement confirmed for me that the team was indeed economically viable. He said the team would not require the new lease to be tied into a season ticket, club seat, or luxury box sales goal as the 1998 lease had been; instead, the team "would assume the risk." In the 1998 lease, the lease could have been terminated during a one-year precontingency period if the community did not purchase a certain percentage of season tickets, club seats, or luxury boxes. Back then, the "Business Backs the Bills" committee, chaired by banker Erkie

Kailbourne, was formed by many local business leaders to ensure the community would meet the sales goals contained in the lease. The committee succeeded in its stated task, as the lease's sales goals were met. We had anticipated the team would again require such a provision, but in our first real negotiation session they took that bargaining chip off the table.

Jeff and Russ discussed that the team's fan base demographic, as it pertained to seats sold, had changed since 1998. They noted the team had acquired many more sponsors in the Rochester area and ticket sales from southern Ontario. In fact, they noted individuals from outside the immediate Buffalo area made up 47 percent of the season ticket base, 65 percent of group sales, and 63 percent of individual game sales. Further, according to Russ, individuals from outside of New York made up 30 percent of the season ticket base, 46 percent of group sales, and 37 percent of individual game sales. In other words, the effort to grow the team's market in southern Ontario and the Toronto series games had been very successful, as an entire new fan base had been created to help underwrite the ticket and club seat sales at Ralph Wilson Stadium.

By taking the potential lease termination clause tied to ticket sales off the table, the Bills reps revealed to me that the team was financially viable, and willing to commit to a lease even if season ticket and luxury box sales dropped. Rich Tobe and I discussed this after the meeting, agreeing that it confirmed that the team was not only economically viable in Buffalo but in fact was doing very well.

Jeff then went into the part of the discussion he knew the State's representatives would be interested in hearing—the amount of revenue New York State derives from the team being located in New York. Jeff noted that with the Jets and Giants being located in New Jersey, the only true New York team was the Bills, and the State greatly benefitted from that. He said that in 2012 the team paid a payroll of approximately $132 million for its New York employees, and because player salaries were growing so much, it was expected to increase by another $15 million for the next year. The report did not detail how they accounted for the aggregate number (i.e., what percentage was salaries for players, coaches, and administrative staff), but at first glance it seemed like an accurate figure, and one the State could confirm by reviewing the records of the State Department of Taxation and Finance.

Jeff then discussed stadium renovations the team would like to see: basic preventative maintenance to extend the stadium's life; additions that would retain the intimacy of attending a game at the Ralph; revitalizing all concessions and bathrooms; easing congestion in concourses and entry and exit points into the stadium, with this portion of the renovations being the largest (and most expensive) part of the project; embracing new technology and upgrading wiring and bandwidth in the facility; and additional high-definition scoreboards in the bowl.

None of these proposed renovations were unexpected. We would have pushed for new bathrooms and concessions if the team had not included them in their wish list, but what surprised us was that there was no mention of more luxury boxes or club seats. I asked if there would be an expectation of construction in this area, and the answer was a definitive no. Russ said the team might actually remove some club seat areas because they believed the team had reached its sales limit.

Jeff stated that the Toronto deal had moved the team "from the fourth to the third quartile of revenue" compared to other teams, but they had probably reached the limit of luxury box sales. He then opened up about the team's viability in Buffalo. He noted the team was and could continue to be viable in western New York as long as a number of factors continued, including the Toronto series. He then broke the Bills viability in Buffalo down to an algebraic equation: $Viability = D \times P^3 - C$.

In the equation, D is demographics, P is passion of the fans, and C is the capital debt expense of the team. In other words, Jeff was saying the team could continue to be very viable in the Buffalo market as long as (1) the demographics of its western New York/southern Ontario fan base continued, (2) the fans were so passionate about their team (hence "passion cubed") they would be willing to pay a standard NFL market rate for the right to see a NFL game in person, and (3) the team did not have a substantial debt load associated with any capital improvements at the stadium or as a result of a new stadium in the future.

Rich and I asked a few questions regarding what the team's representatives felt would be standard market rate for an NFL game. Russ responded that while the team was currently charging below the average market rate, a small growth in prices each year could ensure continued economic viability and success in western New York.

My notes do not indicate any important questions being asked by the State representatives present. While they might have asked a question or two that I don't remember, I do recall that Sam Hoyt told me after the meeting he was relaying all information to his superiors in Albany, but he had not been granted any specific authority at this time to negotiate any terms. This would prove to be a continuing issue and growing problem over the coming months. For now, though, they were there to participate as needed and confirm the governor fully supported the efforts to keep the team in Buffalo.

Jeff then stated the team projected a three-year timeline to complete the renovations: the first year would cover low-risk construction items such as restrooms and concession stands; year two would see large wholesale construction throughout the stadium's concourses and entryways (the "Big Dig," as Jeff called it); and the third year would be the final phase of the Big Dig. At this point we had not yet seen any schematics or drawings of what the second- and third-year renovations would look like, but I remember thinking, "Big Dig means Big Money."

Jeff closed by noting the upcoming league schedule of meetings, and that if the parties could have a memorandum of understanding agreed on by the upcoming training camp it would be possible to have the new lease transaction approved by the other owners at the NFL's fall meeting scheduled for October 2012. He said he would be briefing the NFL's Stadium Committee at its next scheduled meeting on March 5, 2012, and would inform the committee of the discussions held in our present meeting.

At this point we had surpassed our allotted time of two hours for the meeting, and everyone agreed it was a good time to stop. Mary Owen noted the team should be able to provide detailed plans and drawings at the next meeting and the team would bring a representative of the architectural firm Populous to discuss the renovation proposal.

We then handed back our copies of the reports the Bills had brought, and we all shook hands. We all agreed that we were off to a good start on what would surely be a very time- and labor-intensive process.

Of course, I could not see at the time just how intensive the process would be.

Chapter 6

Enter Populous

Contrary to what many people think, negotiations like these are not necessarily a constant conversation. An active period of discussion might be followed by a significant lull, and the period following the February 2012 meeting is a perfect example of such a situation. After the meeting of February 16, no discussions were held by the parties until Rich Tobe received a call from Jeff Littmann during the first week of March notifying him that Populous had completed its renderings and the Bills were ready to present their "ask."

So, on March 15, the parties gathered again in my conference room to review what the Bills had in mind for renovations of the Ralph. Former Bill, Scott Radecic, now an architect with Populous, arrived early to set up a projector in the room. I introduced myself, and we talked about his playing career as a linebacker for the Bills, our alma maters, and the scandal that had engulfed his, Penn State. I could tell the scandal pained Radecic, but it was clear he felt if the charges against Jerry Sandusky were true he must be punished. We moved on from that sordid topic to the matter at hand, and I told him I looked forward to his presentation. He promised I would not be disappointed. I was not expecting disappointment, but sticker shock was a distinct possibility.

Soon we were joined by Sam Hoyt and Steve Gawlik, once again representing the State; Russ Brandon, Jeff Littmann, and Mike Schiavone on behalf of the Bills; and my team of Rich Tobe, Mike Siragusa, John Loffredo, and Elizabeth Burakowski, Rich's economic affairs deputy. As my notes of the meeting state, we were there to review "the Bills' view on the work needed to keep the stadium current."

Scott started the conversation, distributing to the group a fifty-one-page document entitled "Ralph Wilson Stadium & Training Facility." Scott had the same presentation projected on a five-foot-wide cinema-style projector screen we had in my office's conference room (which has since been replaced by a modern large flat-screen monitor that can also be used for secure communications with other governmental agencies in case of an emergency). Flipping through the document, I could see it included all sorts of schematics and drawings of requested changes to the stadium, pictures of happy digitally rendered fans walking around the new facility in their Bills jerseys, and a few spreadsheets.

It was these spreadsheets I was most interested in because I knew from my prior position as an attorney in the private sector that in all likelihood the final page of the presentation describes the totality of the work to be completed and, most important, the cost. Sure enough, on the final page was a spreadsheet titled "Menu & Pricing" that listed a line-by-line description of many different requested projects, the priority of the project as identified by the team, the cost per line item, and the total cost. However, my eye sight was not as strong as it once was, so I had trouble making out some of the words and figures in the small font used.

I had always had good vision and never needed glasses for any purpose until purchasing my first pair of reading glasses not long before. Without my glasses, I could usually read the newspaper, but books or other documents in smaller fonts could be troublesome, especially in poor lighting. Because I was trying not to miss what Scott was saying, looking like I was paying attention while I was really trying to decipher the page, I could not figure it all out.

Unfortunately, I had left my brand-new pair of glasses back in my office. So as Scott started talking about the proposal, I was racking my brain trying to determine how much the total cost of the project would be. Sitting next to me was Mike Siragusa. Mike does not wear glasses, and I wondered if had had better luck reading the spreadsheet. I whispered to him, "Did you read the final page? How much is it?" Mike looked at me and shook his head. At that point, I decided to wait for a break to try to determine the total cost and to just listen to Scott make his presentation.

Scott noted that the presentation did not include just one proposal, but multiple proposals. He stated Populous had a "good base to work from" in regards to the condition of the stadium and that nearly every proposed change was on the exterior or interior concourses. There was no intention to destroy the primary attributes of the current facility, and that started with preserving the great sightlines at the Ralph and making changes that would complement this feature. He noted Populous's recommendations followed the following basic premises: (1) "keep the present fan experience and build on it," and (2) create a stadium that would "match any other facility" in the league.

The presentation on the screen matched the document handed out to us. While Scott started talking about page three of the document, titled "Goals & Priorities" of the team, I had no trouble reading that page because the words were in a large font. The goals and priorities were broken down to those related to the stadium and those related to the training facility. Projects related to the stadium included (1) "extend the physical life of the stadium;" (2) "total freshen up of the stadium;" (3) "improved ingress and egress for fans;" (4) "integration of modern technology;" (5) "updated and increased number of restrooms;" (6) "renovated and expanded concessions;" and (7) "improved broadcast provisions." Those related to the training facility included (1) "larger locker room;" (2) "expanded weight room;" (3) "enhanced food service areas;" (4) "larger equipment area;" (5) "expanded receiving area and loading docks;" and (6) "additional office space."

Looking at this list, nothing really surprised me, though reading all the proposals related to the training facility I started wondering whether we were being asked to support a project geared to the fans or the players. As the presentation continued, I eventually realized it was both.

Scott then directed our attention to the spreadsheet on page four, entitled "Program Brief," which compared the current square feet of the stadium and facility to what it would be if the proposed renovations were implemented in full. At this point I began to realize that the cost of the renovations would be quite high. The project proposed increasing the stadium's square footage from 900,000 to 1,103,273, a nearly 25 percent increase in the stadium's footprint, adding a new West Plaza of 111,264 square feet, building a new operations building of 25,000 square feet, and increasing the training facility by 19,308 square feet.

The spreadsheet also included breakdowns on number of restroom facilities for men and women based on "toilet fixture/person," point-of-sale locations for concessions, and square-footage area in each level for each person. Scott explained differences in the number of men who could use a restroom at one time compared to women, how many more women's toilets were needed now since more women were part of the fan base than before, and the differences in the amount of space needed for toilets, troughs, and urinals. His detailed report included a breakdown of how much space was calculated for use per man at the existing troughs in the restrooms compared to current codes for urinals (for the record, code is twenty-four inches per man at a trough and thirty inches at a urinal). My staff member Liz Burakowski joked out loud that she never would have guessed when she walked into the room that morning she would be getting a lesson on how many men could use a restroom at one time. The rest of us, all men, laughed a bit uncomfortably.

Moving on from the restroom needs of patrons, Scott launched into an explanation of square footage per person for each of the stadium's levels, noting that the Ralph fell far short of the current standard. Anyone who walked through a game at halftime could confirm that fact, as people were jammed in like sardines in a can, making moving around the stadium a slow process. In fact, according to the Bills' analysis, in the 100-level of the stadium, the average square foot per fan was 1.26, compared to the industry standard of 4.3; the 200-level, including the north and south club seats, was 8.12, whereas the standard was 15; and the 300-level was 2.6 compared to a standard of 4.3.

This was perhaps not the most exciting topic to discuss, but I knew any increase in the amount of square footage per fan would be costly because it would require opening up the concourses—which was exactly what the team recommended. The Bills proposed increasing the square footage per person in the 100-level from the then current 1.26 to 3.24, from 8.12 in the 200-level to 14.12, and from 2.6 in the 300-level to 3.81, primarily through greatly increasing concourse width. Though these numbers might sound minor, the cost associated with accomplishing such changes would be huge, and I did not need my reading glasses on to understand this point.

As Scott continued on the subject of the various benefits of increasing the square footage per person in only the way an architect could, my eyes drifted down the spreadsheet to the next section, "Suites," which noted the number of suites in the current facility compared to the one proposed. While 200-level suites would remain the same, at sixty-eight, the number of 100-level suites was proposed to be reduced from seventy-four to fifty-four. We knew the Bills did not sell all the suites on an annual basis, and some were vacant at every game, but we never expected them to want to reduce the number by twenty. This told me the team had probably done the best they could to sell them all but had concluded they could not do it, so it made sense to convert the space for other uses.

Scott confirmed my thought when he explained the suite reduction would allow the team to "repurpose" the space for more productive use. Russ described how many of the 100-level suites dated back to before the improvements related to the 1998 lease renovations and were below the industry standard for size and technology. Additionally, many former 100-level suite owners were now 200-level owners. He suggested it made sense to combine some 100-level suites from two to one and repurpose others for new uses that would enhance the fan experience, especially as it pertained to better concession service.

A few questions were directed to Russ and Scott regarding suite size and whether the team had reached the limit of suite sales. While Scott answered the first question, I don't recall anyone ever truly answering the second. Finishing up this page of the presentation, Scott noted the number of individual seats would not change, and the spreadsheet confirmed the number remained at 68,804.

Scott then began describing the specifics of the proposed renovations. Turning to the next page, I noted thirty-six separate projects listed, ranging from "1. New food court and toilets at 50-yard line" to "36. Add gas-fired radiant heat about sideline club seating." Scott noted the thirty-six projects were broken into four separate "buckets" based on priority as determined by the team. Jeff interrupted to note the first bucket included those solely related to fan amenities, such as upgrading the restrooms and concession stands, as they were the highest priority requests from fans. I felt that Jeff was saying this to imply that while there was a lot there for the team, they put fans' requests ahead of their own when it came to prioritizing the projects.

For the remainder of the presentation we looked at architectural renderings of before and after drawings of how the stadium and training facility would look if the renovations were completed: where concourses would be opened up, where new restroom and concession facilities would be located, how this impacted water, utility, and other equipment lines, how the main administration and training building would be expanded, and so on. By this time in the meeting, no specific number had been stated for the cost of the proposed renovations. I knew the number was on the last page but could not make it out. The suspense was killing me, especially since I knew the others—at least those with better eye sight than mine or wearing glasses—already knew the number.

Finally, after almost two hours without a break, we reached the final page describing all of the projects, prioritized in the four "buckets" with the individual price tag for each project listed, the combined price per bucket, and the total price for the entire proposed renovation. Scott clicked his laptop's presentation wireless remote and, projected on the wall screen, the number in the bottom right corner of the spreadsheet finally became clear: $210,273,000.

I knew going in that the total amount would be large, but I really wasn't sure what kind of number to expect after Jeff had said at the last meeting that the team was not contemplating a major retrofit similar to what Kansas City and Green Bay had done. The final price tag to retrofit Arrowhead Stadium had been about $375 million. Considering the $210 million price tag for our proposed renovations, I could appreciate the difference in the dollar amount, yet the proposed projects remained quite large—perhaps large enough to be considered "retrofit-light."

Now that I could read the final page, I could see the four buckets of projects were split up as follows: (1) fan-based renovations, including concession and restroom updates, and general maintenance in the total amount of $25,473,000; (2) general facility upgrades, including pushing out fence line and construction of new gates, renovating suites, installing new high-definition scoreboards, upgrading the training facility, and building a new operations and storage building, for a combined total of $58,101,000; (3) new facilities and repurposing of space to create new cooking areas for concessions, relocating the press box, renovating certain areas to create new concessions and lounge space, rewiring the entire stadium, and other smaller adjustments, for a combined cost of $53,376,000; and (4) expanding the concourses and creating new clubs and concourse food courts on both sides of the fifty-yard lines, for the meager sum of $73,323,000. As I had surmised, expanding the concourses would be quite costly, and I was right—it was the most expensive bucket and line item project.

After reviewing the presentation, it became apparent to me that while the team's representatives had said they were not interested in an Arrowhead-scale retrofit, their proposals pretty much indicated a retrofit was really what they wanted. No matter what it was called, if the County and State were to agree to such a large proposal, the Bills would have to agree to a long-term commitment to the facility. In other words, everything presented was subject to negotiation.

While I was focusing on the cost of the "retrofit-light" renovations, Scott mentioned how the proposed renovations could not be completed in one off-season, but in fact could take up to three years to complete. Year one would be spent modernizing and renovating the restrooms, concessions, and administrative and training buildings; year two would be devoted to major structural modifications to open up the concourses; and in year three concourse work and clean-up of smaller projects would be completed. Scott closed his portion of the presentation by offering to answer any questions on the architectural aspects of the proposed renovations, of which there were a few from the County and State's teams.

After Scott answered the questions, Jeff Littmann finished speaking on behalf of the team by noting Mr. Wilson had been and still was committed to Buffalo and believed the "time [was] right to upgrade the stadium to make it competitive for many years to come." Jeff stated, "Right now, the team can't compete on the economic scale with other teams" but, if implemented in full, "this proposal would do that." He then thanked us for our time and asked if anyone had further questions.

I thanked Jeff, Russ, and Scott for their presentation and commended Mr. Wilson for his commitment to the area. I noted that no one on the County's team questioned Mr. Wilson's commitment to the area, and this proposal indicated to me that the team intended on playing at the Ralph for many years to come. I noted the significant price tag for the proposals, and that this would be an extremely large expense for the governmental entities before we could even start discussing other costs, such as operating, working capital, and game-day expenses.

The only question I had at this time, directed to Jeff, was whether the Bills intended to contribute toward the cost of renovation and, if so, to what degree. I did not expect a yes or no at the moment and asked Jeff to take the question back to Mr. Wilson and provide both the County and State teams an answer at our next meeting. I assume Jeff expected the question would be forthcoming, perhaps not at this meeting, but soon enough. Talking with Rich Tobe before the meeting, we agreed it would be fair to ask the question if the Bills' presentation included a price tag for the work proposed. Considering the $210 million price tag was presented, it made sense to make the request now rather than wait until the next meeting and delay the negotiations.

And I wanted to ask the question in person, rather than over the phone or by email. Having completed many, many negotiations over the years, first as an attorney, then as county comptroller, and now as county executive, I understand the benefits of asking the opposing side a difficult question face to face: first, to show the other side you're not afraid to negotiate a tough position in person, and second, to gauge the response from the other side.

When I asked the question, I did not blink, and neither did Jeff when he said it was a fair question, one he would discuss with Mr. Wilson and get back to us. Jeff's reputation as a tough negotiator was proving true, but I wanted to show him that I was willing to be tough and drive a hard bargain as well.

As had happened in February, Sam Hoyt and Steve Gawlik did not say much during the meeting. They asked an occasional question, and at the end Sam said they would take all the information discussed back to their bosses in Albany and New York City. When Sam said this, I could see the disappointment on the faces of the Bills representatives. I have known Sam and Steve for many years. I respect both, as well as their abilities at the negotiating table. But they were in a difficult position in that they did not have the authority to negotiate on behalf of the State. They could relay information back to the governor's office and the Empire State Development Corporation's offices in Albany and New York City, but not much could be accomplished until the State became more intimately involved. I was starting to get a bit impatient with the State's inaction. I could only imagine what the Bills were thinking at that point, and from the looks on their faces it was not good.

We all shook hands, and I thanked Scott for his detailed presentation. The meeting concluded with one change from the prior meeting's end: there was no request by the Bills to return the documents we were provided. I'm sure the Bills expected the schematics, drawings, and spreadsheets to end up in the hands of the local media in time for the evening's newscast. However, in fact, at no time did the County or the State give these reports, drawings, or future drawings to a reporter.

I told my staff that if any document was released to the media I would find out who did it and there would be serious repercussions, including possible termination. I did this to show the Bills and the State they could trust the County's team not to leak confidential—or for that matter, nonconfidential—information provided during negotiating sessions. And that is what happened: at no time did these architectural renderings or spreadsheets ever reach the public eye.

Unlike many other governments, where it seems middle- and even high-level employees live to be the unnamed source in a news article, I am proud to say no one from my team revealed any secrets to media members. While this drove the Buffalo media crazy, and led to incessant questions regarding the status of negotiations, it proved to the Bills team we could be trusted, which in turn led to more productive discussions. We set that standard early in our discussions and maintained it throughout. In the end, I believe this helped solidify the trust needed among parties in order for a successful conclusion to our negotiations to occur.

Chapter 7

G4 or 4G?

The March meeting was again followed by a lull in negotiations among parties. In fact, no real negotiations occurred for more than two months—but that does not mean nothing was accomplished during this time. In fact, the period between the March 15, 2012, meeting and our next meeting on May 25 was one of the most important periods for the County because it was then that we really learned the intricacies surrounding the NFL's G4 financing program.

G4, or 4G as Rich Tobe and I mistakenly called it for a few weeks (as if it were the latest in mobile phone technology), was the newly adopted stadium construction financing program for the league. It was so new, in fact, that it had yet to be used in any stadium renovation or new construction deal. At the County level we knew very little about it, other than hearing such a program existed and that it replaced the former G3 program. If you had asked any member of the County's team to describe the terms of the program, you would have received a blank stare in response.

In short order we knew a great deal about the program, however. On March 29, Rich Tobe, Mike Siragusa, and I were joined by Sam Hoyt and Steve Gawlik as our outside counsel from Nixon Peabody provided a tutorial on the G4 program and recent stadium transactions. Chris Melvin, Martha Anderson, and Liz Columbo from Nixon met the group in my conference room and, after the State's team gave instructions to Nixon's representatives, Chris began the discussion highlighting what he had learned from attending the most recent NFL owner's meeting.

This is where our choice of Nixon as outside counsel started to bear fruit—no other local firm's attorney had the contacts in the league that Chris Melvin had. He could speak not only from his experience closing prior deals, but also from attending the owners' meetings and knowing the players in the NFL's main office. While Martha Anderson and Liz Columbo had the transactional experience from closing prior sports teams' stadiums transactions, Chris had the "boots on the ground" knowledge from attending and getting to know the parties in the NFL. This knowledge proved invaluable.

Chris noted the talk at the recent owners' meeting was not about moving a team, but possible expansion candidates were discussed. He described how two competing factions were interested in bringing a team to the Los Angeles market: representatives from the City of Industry, California, and those for a more central location. He felt that while other owners were receptive to a possible third shot for a team in LA, it was doubtful any action would be taken because ownership of a franchise would have to be solidified, something that had not really happened yet, and also because a new stadium would have to be built. While all sorts of discussions took place about potential sites for a new stadium, in reality such a move was years from occurring, if it ever occurred at all. Chris believed the NFL would not move a current franchise to LA unless the stadium issue had been resolved.

Additionally, Chris noted any owner seeking to move a team to Los Angeles would inevitably have to pay a relocation fee of perhaps $300 million to the league in addition to paying the extraordinary costs associated with constructing a new stadium. Hearing these facts helped settle some nerves we had regarding the possibility of Mr. Wilson passing away and an LA interest swooping in to buy the team and moving it before we could close our new deal. If it appeared LA was off the table for now, it would make our life much easier in case the unforeseen should happen before we inked a new lease term.

Chris then gave us a tutorial on the most recent stadium deal entered into—Levi's Stadium for the San Francisco 49ers in Santa Clara, California. Chris noted the deal allowed for two teams to use the stadium, similar to Pittsburgh's stadium deal in which the Steelers and University of Pittsburgh Panthers shared the field. However, Chris said the terms of the Santa Clara deal were not advantageous for the second team because all the real benefits flowed to the 49ers.

Chris noted construction costs for the stadium were expected to surpass $1 billion, and while the City of Santa Clara provided a subsidy, the vast majority of construction costs were to be privately paid and then offset under the older G3 program's seat license fee. In fact, when the seat license fees were revealed, it became apparent there was no comparison to what was being built in Santa Clara and what we were attempting to do in renovating the Ralph. While it was questionable whether seat licenses could be sold in the Buffalo market, licenses were being sold in the new Levi's Stadium for $80,000 per seat between the forty-yard lines in the lower bowl. Even "nose bleed" seats did not come cheap—$2,000 per seat for merely *the right* to buy 49ers season tickets.

While a few questions were asked, we all realized that not much could be learned from this latest stadium deal—just as nothing could be learned from the recent renovations at the Meadowlands in New Jersey by the Giants and Jets, a project that was 100 percent paid for by the teams. The closest comparison we had was to Lucas Oil Stadium in Indianapolis. While the Colts organization was obligated for $100 million of liability toward the construction, we were told in fact that it was the State and County governments that paid the full price tag of nearly $700 million for its construction. Even this comparison was not too helpful, however, as it was for the construction of a new stadium and was completed under the NFL's financing program then in use, which was a precursor to G3. When it came to the G4 program, the lease deal we were negotiating would be the first to be applied under the new system.

Chris and Martha then discussed what they knew of the G4 program: (1) the NFL would provide a two-for-one match on any dollars spent by the owner, not a third party or a government, through a loan; (2) at least $50 million must be spent on the project; (3) sufficient new revenue streams would have to be created to justify the capital expense, with revenues used to repay the loan to the league; and (4) the NFL's portion of G4 financing would have to be repaid in full upon the sale of a team.

While this was about as much information as anyone outside of the league office knew, it was very helpful to us as we moved forward in negotiations. We now knew there was an incentive for the team to spend its own money on the construction so they could leverage potentially twice as much as they put in from the league. This information also revealed to us why the team, if it pursued such a G4 option, would inevitably seek new forms of revenue from such construction. We now knew why the Bills proposed in the March meeting to update all concession stands with new point-of-sale machines—new machines meant you could accept credit cards, which would inevitably lead to new revenue. It also explained why a new team store was part of the construction wish list—a new store on Abbott Road meant many thousands, perhaps millions, of dollars more in sales of merchandise that would benefit the team and league through shared revenue.

Knowing all this helped us understand why the Bills organization was proposing some items on their list and also how we would respond to those requests. I realized if we were to strike out these portions of the project, it would limit the team's ability to participate in the G4 program, thereby meaning the team would contribute fewer dollars for the other portions of the project we really wanted. Without counsel from Chris Melvin and his team, we would not have known about this and might have acted in a way that could have hurt what we were trying to accomplish: getting a new lease deal done in which the team paid for a significant portion of the construction costs. Picking the right counsel matters.

After about two hours of discussions, I thanked Chris, Martha, and Liz for their counsel, and we wrapped up the meeting. What we did not discuss in the meeting was the negotiating stance we wanted to take with Nixon now on board. We invited Sam Hoyt and Steve Gawlik to attend this meeting, as we were to discuss the NFL's financing programs and we felt it was important for the State's team to understand it as well, but we did not want to reveal any specifics of the County's negotiation strategy while the State's representatives were present.

That discussion would be held during a phone conference on May 25 when Chris Melvin, Martha Anderson, and Liz Columbo joined Rich Tobe, Mike Siragusa, John Loffredo, Liz Burakowski, and myself. This discussion was not on G3, G4, or any other financing program, but rather on how we should approach the next meeting between all of the parties, which was now scheduled for May 29.

As the last meeting in March was the Bills' opportunity to make its presentation on what it proposed the project should entail, this meeting was now our chance to respond. Of primary concern was what question we should start with: a discussion on the items proposed, or whether the Bills were willing to contribute to the costs? Chris suggested we start right with whether the team would contribute because, for one, I had asked Jeff Littmann to take the question back to Mr. Wilson for his consideration at our last meeting, and two, the existence of the G4 program meant there was no real reason for the team to say no.

We then established the parameters of how the question would be asked, who would ask it, and what our response would be. We all agreed I would ask the question directly to Jeff, and if he said yes, we would continue onward. However, if he said no, I was to immediately show my disgust by telling them that answer was unacceptable, picking up my materials, and walking out of the meeting, leaving the others to pick up the pieces.

If the team was not willing to contribute to the construction, I was not going to waste my time sitting around the table pleading for the Bills to contribute a few dollars to the overall cost. In my mind—and the rest of our negotiating team agreed—the team was either a partner going forward or there would be no deal. We were not going to be a patsy, taking whatever scraps we were offered. While this was a risky strategy, it was the only way to let the team know we were serious. My walking out would send a message to the team as well as the State's representatives that the County was willing to play hardball.

With that important point settled, we spent the rest of the phone conference reviewing matters we would have to address in the discussions: new ground rules, the length of the lease, a non-relocation agreement, funding categories (game-day expenses, annual operating expenses, annual capital expenses, etc.), the Toronto series, naming rights, other uses of the stadium and its facilities (such as the fieldhouse), and every other matter that even tangentially touched the stadium.

Pertaining to the length of the lease, we told the Nixon Peabody representatives we would be quite happy with a fifteen-year lease, though we were asking for a twenty-year term. We knew by asking for a twenty-year lease we were telegraphing to the Bills we would accept a lesser term, but when it comes to negotiations you have to start somewhere to eventually reach the term that's acceptable to you. Any term short of ten years was unacceptable. A ten- to fifteen-year lease would be satisfactory depending on the other terms, especially if we received an ironclad non-relocation agreement. Any term of fifteen years or more would be acceptable as long as no buyout provision existed, as in the terms of the 1998 lease.

We then reviewed an analysis completed by my office and verified by Nixon Peabody beforehand showing all renovation projects completed for NFL stadiums from 1990 onward, the cost of the project, the team's and league's contribution toward the construction costs, if any, and what percentage of each renovation deal the team and the league paid for in each case. Our analysis showed that from 1990 to 1999, four renovation projects had taken place: Jacksonville in 1995, Oakland in 1996, San Diego in 1997, and Buffalo in 1999. Of these four transactions, the only one in which the owner and league participated in the construction costs was in Jacksonville, and only for 10 percent of the cost ($13 million of a $130 million project). In the other three, neither the team nor the league contributed toward construction costs.

However, our analysis revealed that starting with the Green Bay transaction in 2001, the team and the league started to contribute a significant share of the renovation construction costs. In Green Bay, the team and the league paid $126 million of the $295 million project, or 42.71 percent. In Chicago in 2003, the team and the league contributed $250 million of a $660 million project, or $37.88 percent. In Kansas City in 2010, the team and the league contributed $125 million of the $375 million project, or one-third of the total cost.

In the two most recent renovations, New Orleans in 2011 and Tampa Bay in 2012, neither the team nor the league contributed any sum, but we discounted these transactions because they were much smaller in total size: $86 million total for New Orleans, and $8 million for Tampa Bay.

Thus, using the Green Bay, Chicago, and Kansas City renovations as the baseline averages for our transaction, we determined the team and league recent "average" for construction-cost contribution for a stadium to be 37.67 percent. That is not to say we were expecting the

Bills to pay approximately 37 percent of the construction costs; we were going to use this as a bargaining chip to get whatever we could out of the team. We knew anything greater than the prior contribution of zero would be a win for our side, considering the team previously paid nothing in the 1998 lease transaction. Yet, we really hoped to get the team and the league to contribute approximately one-third of the construction costs.

Rich Tobe prepared a two-page, single-spaced agenda for our use during this phone conference, and this was how we approached every future meeting among all parties. Rich would prepare the agenda and then send it to Jeff Littmann for his review and concurrence. This had a dual purpose: it allowed us to set the agenda, and it revealed to Jeff the topics we wished to discuss without going into detail or revealing our strategy, thereby giving him some comfort going into the meeting that the parties were headed in the right direction. While we might never get to every topic listed on the agenda, it set the tone for the meeting and prioritized the important issues over the lesser ones.

After spending what seemed like an entire day on the teleconference, we finished the call agreeing we were more than prepared for the next meeting in four days, and hoping I would not have to walk out less than a minute or two after the meeting started.

Chapter 8

Should I Stay or Should I Go?

When I walked into my office on May 29, 2012, I realized that day could make or break not only the lease negotiations but my entire administration. If I walked out of negotiations, I expected word to percolate to the press by the end of the day from either the Bills' or State's team that I walked out, signifying things were going badly. If that happened, I fully anticipated a chorus of criticism to be hurled at me from both the press and the general public.

I hoped I would not have to face such a scenario, but I was set to face it if necessary. I have learned over the years that once you are perceived as being weak during any negotiations, it is highly doubtful you will ever achieve what you are seeking. While walking out would be a risk, it was a risk I was willing to take to get the best deal I could for the County, and therefore the greater community.

Prior to the meeting I sat down for a few minutes with Rich Tobe and Mike Siragusa. Rich and I went over the order of the agenda. We decided not to ask the question that was looming immediately upon my first statement. Instead we decided to confirm before everyone the basic ground rules of the negotiations and then ask the question. Mike confided in me that he was glad he was not in my shoes and hoped my shoes, with me in them, would not have to walk out of the conference room alone. With that, at 2 p.m. the meeting began in my office's executive conference room. This time, I brought my reading glasses with me.

The room was as full for this meeting as for any other gathering I had held there, besides my monthly department head and commissioner meetings. Representing the Bills were Jeff Littmann, Russ Brandon, Mary Owen, Mike Schiavone, and Eugene Driker, Mr. Wilson's personal attorney. The County was once again represented by myself, Rich Tobe, Mike Siragusa, John Loffredo, and Liz Burakowski, but for this meeting we were joined by Chris Melvin, Martha Anderson, and Liz Columbo of Nixon Peabody. The State's team—Sam Hoyt and Steve Gawlik—had not changed, though everyone in the room knew they had no real authority to negotiate on behalf of the Cuomo Administration and were there to basically take notes and report back to someone above them.

Using the agenda Rich Tobe had prepared, I opened the meeting by going over the basic ground rules the parties had earlier agreed to in principle: no issue was deemed agreed upon until the entire deal was complete; personal discussions, in person or by phone, would be used by all to try to achieve a consensus; all forms of assistance would be considered as part of the deal; and the final deal should be based on past terms used by the parties but be comparable to other deals of similar type recently negotiated (this was a reference to the other recent stadium renovation analysis discussed during our May 25, 2012, phone conference with Nixon Peabody).

Though I knew everyone had agreed to these basic ground rules in our private conversations, it was helpful to have everyone personally agree to the principles in front of the others again. It provided a level of assurance that we could agree to these basic broad principles, making it easier to agree in the end on the minute details.

After everyone had agreed to the ground rules, I looked straight at Jeff and asked him to answer the question I had posed at the prior meeting: was Mr. Wilson willing to contribute toward the capital infrastructure costs associated with the proposed project—and if so, how much?

I vividly remember hearing at that moment the voice of Mick Jones of The Clash singing the lyrics to their hit "Should I Stay or Should I Go" in my head. I really did think, as Jones sings, "if I go, there will be trouble," because I knew if I left it would signal a breakdown in talks. However, I knew if I stayed it would not "be double," as Jones sang in the song. So I was hoping for a positive response from Jeff.

Jeff answered the first part of the question quickly, stating, "The team is willing to contribute toward a share of the construction costs." On hearing this, I did not outwardly smile, but I was very relieved that I did not have to resort to the nuclear option of showing my disgust and walking out.

However, although Jeff had given me the answer I had hoped to hear regarding the first part of my question, he really did not answer the second part and instead started to add a few provisos to his answer. Though the team was willing to contribute toward the cost of construction, he said, we should not be making an "apples to apples comparison on team to team costs." Hearing this did not surprise me. I assumed this was Jeff's way of saying "you probably have completed an analysis of other recent stadium renovations and know that some teams have contributed a significant amount toward the overall costs; however, each project is different and needs to viewed independently."

Jeff then noted the team had incurred an "8.6 percent increase" in costs above and beyond what was expected and agreed to in the 1999 lease due to issues related to greater security and code compliance initiatives that had to be put in place following September 11, 2001, requirements of the Americans with Disabilities Act, and higher than projected utility expenses. He stated this increase totaled about $10 million annually. Jeff said while the team might not have contributed toward the original renovation construction costs negotiated during the lease, the team did in fact incur significant annual infrastructure costs that were not contemplated during the prior negotiations and this was part of "Mr. Wilson's commitment to keeping the team in Buffalo and Western New York."

Continuing, Jeff said they wanted to use the basic blueprint of the prior deal as it pertained to the retention of architectural and engineering firms for the project, with which we had previously agreed. The team's goal was to have the construction start upon the conclusion of the 2012–2013 season, and for that to happen we would need to reach an agreement prior to the October NFL owners' meeting, as any agreement was subject to the approval by the fellow owners.

While I did not foresee an issue with that date from the County's end, if New York State did not begin to take the negotiations seriously, I could not imagine how a deal could be completed ahead of the owners' meeting. I think this was Jeff's way of telling Sam and Steve it was time to ramp-up negotiations from the State's end. Otherwise the project's construction schedule would be jeopardized.

Jeff then surprised everyone in the room. "Ralph Wilson's goal," he said, "is to get a deal done that preserves the team in Buffalo, and he is willing to commit to repay the full investment made by the governmental entities if the team moves." I had been writing down some of what Jeff said on my notepad, and continued to do so while he said this, all the while thinking to myself this sounds great, but it anticipates the possibility of the team moving during the term of the lease, which would be a disaster.

Rich asked Jeff what exactly Mr. Wilson meant by committing to repay the "full investment." Did he mean the State's and County's construction costs associated with the new lease? Or did he mean all costs associated with the stadium? Jeff responded it meant repaying the County and State for any construction costs incurred as a result of the new lease if the team moved prior to the new lease's expiration.

This surprised me. Jeff was essentially implying that Mr. Wilson intended to keep the team in Buffalo, but that there was a significant chance the team might move following his death. While the pledge to repay the governments their portion of construction costs was appreciated, I knew it did not really matter how much we got paid if the team moved because the community would suffer in the end with the loss of our team.

Jeff then stated the team's commitment to contribute to the construction costs was predicated on meeting the standards of a "new financing program" instituted by the NFL: G4. Having just received a tutorial on the G4 program from Chris Melvin during our recent conference call, much of what Jeff described I was familiar with. However, he added a few details that perhaps Chris did not even know: (1) the program required all construction to be completed within a thirty-month timeline, though the team had planned on a three-year construction period; and (2) the loan repayment program required the increased revenue to exist for up to fifteen years.

Jeff also emphasized a term Chris had told us about: that a change in ownership required immediate repayment of the NFL's portion of the loan. His highlighting of this term once again accentuated the possibility of Mr. Wilson not being the owner at some point during the term of the next lease. While this might not seem a strange comment to make considering Mr. Wilson's advanced age at the time, it was an affirmation by the team's representatives of Mr. Wilson's mortality and the possibility of a new owner acquiring the team during the lease term. Further, Rich had told me several times that during the 1999 lease negotiation there was never a single reference to the potential death of Mr. Wilson and the subsequent transfer of the team—there was only Mr. Wilson.

So in just a few sentences, Jeff Littmann reiterated Mr. Wilson's pledge to keep the team in Buffalo but, without saying so directly, hinted at Mr. Wilson's mortality and the odds he would not survive whatever term we agreed upon in the new lease, and offered to repay the State of New York and Erie County for any future expenses we should incur to renovate Ralph Wilson Stadium if the team should thereafter move.

A key to good negotiating is to be able to anticipate your opponent's arguments and offers so that when they're made you're prepared to respond. I have to admit I was a bit surprised by the offer to repay the governments for the future debt-service costs. As I originally thought, it sounds great but indicates the possibility the team could move from Buffalo, the least desirable future result. My goal entering into these negotiations was to get a long-term ironclad lease that prohibited the team from moving, or at least made a move so onerous that it was doubtful the team would ever move even if it could legally do so. While I may not have anticipated the offer, I immediately realized its significance.

Mr. Wilson had said during recent years he had no intention of either moving the team or selling it during his lifetime. He honored both of those commitments. He also said the team would be sold after his death. However, the question that had gone unanswered was whether any stipulation had been placed upon Mr. Wilson's death requiring the team to be kept in Buffalo. Jeff's offer now appeared to answer this question in the negative.

As negotiations commenced, Rich told me Jeff had hinted to him in conversations that Mr. Wilson had already placed his shares of Buffalo Bills, Inc. (the team's corporate structure) in a trust he controlled. As an attorney who had prepared trust documents for former clients,

I knew a trust can be drafted in any way possible to meet the wishes of the owner upon his or her transfer of the trust's assets to the trust. Depending on how the trust is drafted, the trust might also offer many tax savings for the owner during the owner's lifetime. To get the best tax savings, an owner of an asset usually must give up all current control of the asset, including future use and control of the asset.

In other words, Mr. Wilson probably already transferred his shares of Buffalo Bills, Inc., to a trust, controlled by independent trustees who could keep, sell, give, or otherwise dispose of the trust's assets as the trustees saw fit unless Mr. Wilson put certain stipulations on the transfer of the team in the trust document.

We assumed Mr. Wilson included provisions in the trust that prohibited the sale of the team during his lifetime. However, through Jeff Littmann's offer to pay back the governments our future infrastructure costs if the team moved, it confirmed to us that no such provision restricting the sale of the team after Mr. Wilson's death existed in his trust. If Mr. Wilson had included a provision in the trust requiring the team to stay in Buffalo, there would be no reason to offer to repay the governments for our future infrastructure costs. So, without directly telling us, Jeff Littmann let the proverbial cat out of the bag that the team not only would be put up for sale upon Mr. Wilson's death, but that there were no provisions requiring the new owner to keep the team in Buffalo.

I do not know if it was intentional, but the Bills were doing us a favor by revealing the team could be moved once it was sold. It confirmed in my mind that the most important term to the upcoming lease was not which set of projects out of the four buckets presented at the last meeting needed to be completed, or worrying about every cent spent on the project, but getting a lease that included terms so onerous a new owner could not move the team.

Jeff's revelation also directly pivoted into a discussion on the length of the new lease's term and any non-relocation provisions we sought. I stated that while I appreciated the offer to repay the County for our capital infrastructure costs if the team moved, I was more interested in ensuring the team did not move. I said, "The best way to protect the public's investment at Ralph Wilson Stadium is not to repay us upon the team moving but to ensure the team never moves."

My goal was to secure a lease that ensured the long-term viability of the Buffalo Bills, not a franchise that would eventually become the Los Angeles Bills or Toronto Bills. In my view, the best way to accomplish this was with a non-relocation agreement to be included in the final documents. That is exactly what I asked for, though the Bills' negotiation team did not respond at the time.

At this point in the negotiations I do not think either side was ready to engage in full-blown negotiations at the bargaining table, so to speak. Rather, we were listening to the other's requests and contemplating them to respond at a later date. At the March 29, 2012, meeting the Bills made their presentation on what renovations they hoped to complete at the Ralph as part of the new lease. At this session we sought an assurance on the basic ground rules and an opportunity to discuss the terms we felt were required for the County to agree to a new lease.

The fact was that while the Bills' and the County's negotiating teams were prepared to bargain, the State was not. It really did not matter what either the Bills or the County put on the table at this point because without the State's concurrence nothing could be resolved. And at this point in the discussions the State was really not involved. While Sam Hoyt and Steve Gawlik tried to portray the appearance of being active participants in the discussions, they were not, and everyone at the conference table knew it, including Sam and Steve. I did not begrudge Sam or Steve. They were like lieutenants or colonels on the battlefield taking orders and reporting back to their generals. However, now it was time for the generals to act.

We discussed a few more issues related to the lease, including the need to revise the security protocols before the first preseason game under the final year of the then current lease, as well as the potential to phase the construction over two years, rather than three, and then we wrapped up the talks. We agreed it was another productive session, shook hands, and agreed to schedule another negotiation session in two or three weeks. Russ stated the Bills would like to host the next round of talks at the stadium, which I said was more than agreeable, especially considering we were starting to reach the seating capacity limit of my conference room.

After the meeting, Russ and I talked briefly out of earshot of the others. Russ confided in me his and Jeff's growing aggravation with the failure of State officials to take seriously the talks and the apparent lack of authority of Sam and Steve to make a decision for the State. I told him I understood their position and would relay their feelings to the governor the next time I spoke to him.

I think Sam knew what we were talking about because after the Bills' team had left he approached me and said he and Steve were relaying everything back to members of the governor's staff at the "highest levels" and that he in fact had talked to the governor himself about the negotiations in the past week. I think I rolled my eyes when I heard the "highest levels" and responded by saying that it really did not matter what levels he was talking to because if the State did not start taking the discussions seriously, the negotiations would break down and all fingers would be pointed at the State.

I told Sam I would be reaching out to the governor myself to relay this message and hoped the State would be ready to fully engage in negotiations at the next session. He said he understood and, in fact, was sort of imploring me to do so. He said I should talk to not just the governor but other senior members of his staff. I took this as a sign that while the governor understood the need to complete a lease, other members of his staff did not.

After Sam left, I went back to my office and discussed the round of talks with my team. I noted how I went into the meeting ready to walk out if necessary, thereby putting the lease talks in jeopardy, and now the lease talks were not progressing because the State was fumbling the ball. In less than three hours, the State government had become the stumbling block that I had been willing to be. I much preferred my new position. Now if the press reported that talks were not going anywhere, it was the State that would receive the blame, not me. Regardless, I knew in the long run if we failed to close a deal before the lease expired, or Mr. Wilson passed, we all would be blamed for the failure, and that was an option I was unwilling to accept.

Chapter 9

Percoco

Joe Percoco was a name mentioned in hushed tones in Albany and New York City, though until recently most New Yorkers had never heard of him. Joe was probably the most powerful New Yorker not named Andrew M. Cuomo. Joe Percoco was the gatekeeper to the governor, and he closely guarded the gate.

When it comes to the governor's inner circle, no one was more inside than Joe Percoco. Joe and I met when Andrew Cuomo ran for governor in 2002. At that point, Governor Cuomo had not yet been elected to any political office and was running in a primary for New York governor against the then sitting state comptroller, H. Carl McCall. Carl McCall was popular and also an African American. No African American had ever served as governor, and McCall had secured the support of many Democratic Party leaders from across the state. Realizing he would not win the primary, Cuomo dropped out just before it was held, thereby securing the possibility of running for higher office in the future. I did not really know Joe then.

In 2006, when I was in my first year as Erie County Comptroller and Cuomo was seeking the office of attorney general against other highly qualified individuals, I really became acquainted with Joe Percoco. From my contacts in Albany and New York City, I knew Joe's reputation was one of steadfast loyalty to Cuomo. Additionally, if you wanted to talk to Cuomo, you needed to talk to Joe first. Since my initial meeting with Joe, nothing had changed in that regard.

Over the years, Joe and I have agreed on many issues and dis-agreed on many others, but we've always been able to work out our differences in a mutually acceptable manner. I respected Joe in that he was (and probably still is) loyal to his boss and, unlike what some might say, he is willing to hear an alternative viewpoint and change his view. I knew if I wanted to influence the governor's thought on the Bills lease, I needed first to talk to Joe.

Additionally, Rich Tobe had told me he had heard from his contacts in Albany that some key members of the governor's staff thought there was no need to rush the lease negotiations because the lease did not expire until summer of 2013. Hearing this surprised us, as we thought we had sufficiently argued the need to start the talks now, primarily because of the age of Mr. Wilson.

So when it came to getting the State to be a more active participant in the lease talks, I knew I had to speak to Joe, not necessarily just the governor—who would always take my calls—because Joe, better than anyone, could get the governor to focus on the issue. So two days after the May 29 meeting, I called Joe. I wanted to express my displeasure in the failure of the State to be a more active participant in our discussions, and I wanted to let the governor know if any party was accused of dropping the ball on the talks, it was the State.

Joe and I had a short talk. I let him know in no uncertain terms that although talks were being held, they were going nowhere because the State might as well have not been there. I told him it appeared to all parties that Sam Hoyt and Steve Gawlik had no authority to negotiate for the State and we were going to have to put the talks on hold until the State took the talks seriously.

Joe said Sam and Steve kept the governor informed of the talks and relayed the substance of the talks to other members of the administration. He said the governor took the talks and the future of the team in Buffalo seriously. Joe then confirmed the rumor we had heard: that some members of the administration did not see the need for in-depth negotiations now because the current lease still had another year on it.

At this point I reminded Joe of Mr. Wilson's age and that if Mr. Wilson should die prior to the expiration of the current lease, it is quite possible the team could be sold to a new owner who moved the team either during the final year of the lease or thereafter. After saying this,

I heard what I considered to be a good thing on the other end of the line: silence. Then Joe said, "I'll get back to you."

Joe's a fighter, and a damn good one at that. When you talk through issues with him, he is usually quick with a response. I know when you get Joe thinking of the ramifications of an issue, and how the path being taken by the administration might not be the best one for them, his gruff exterior will disappear and he will listen to your position. In my view, Joe's brief silence was golden because it indicated that he realized that perhaps they were taking the wrong path. And when he said, "I'll get back to you," it meant he would discuss the matter with the governor, and soon.

I hung up not necessarily expecting a call from the governor, but thinking we might see a change in tactics from the State.

A day or two following my talk with Joe, I ran into Sam Hoyt at an event. Sam said he spoke to Joe and told me, "Whatever you told him had him talking about the Bills lease." I took this as a good sign and anticipated a change in the State's participation in the talks.

Chapter 10

The More Things Change,
the More They Remain the Same

While the next round of face-to-face talks was scheduled for June 18, 2012, by this time in the process it was not uncommon for Jeff Littmann and Rich Tobe to speak to each other regularly on the phone, and for all parties to communicate frequently via email. In fact, because the State was in essence a no-show in the process, the only way to move the negotiation along was through these conversations.

So, following the May 29 meeting, the County and the Bills started to share data and information through email on an almost daily basis. On May 31, Jeff Littmann mailed to Rich Tobe and Sam Hoyt copies of the NFL's 2011 resolution creating the G4 program and the 2012 amendment to it. On June 1, Jeff emailed Rich (though not Sam) copies of relevant legal documents relating to the original lease for the stadium.

On June 1, Rich and I discussed sending a new list of outstanding issues to be resolved to the Bills and the State, knowing full well the State would probably not respond, but this would advance the process as it pertained to the team. With June 1 being a Friday, Rich agreed to work on the new list over the weekend so we could send it to the parties on Monday the fourth. He was good to his word—when I arrived at my office on Monday, June 4, there was an email from Rich in my inbox containing a draft for Mike Siragusa, Liz Burakowski, and myself to review. After offering some suggestions, Rich emailed Jeff Littmann, copying the County's negotiating team and Sam Hoyt, the "draft issues list," requesting that Jeff add whatever items he thought should be added.

While, not surprisingly, we did not hear back from the State immediately, on June 8, Rich and Jeff had a long phone conversation. In some ways, more was accomplished by Rich and Jeff during that call than had been in prior meetings. According to Rich's notes of the call, which he emailed to the County's team, but not to the State, on June 9, the first thing Jeff stated was that the "negotiating sessions would be more productive if the number of people present [was] reduced somewhat." While not a definitive critique of the State's lack of participation, both Rich and I took this as the Bills' frustration at the lack of progress and failure of the State to be a productive party.

Jeff also noted that "conversations between meetings should be held to advance issues and understandings." Rich and Jeff had built a level of trust dating back to the 1998 lease negotiations. They knew each other and believed more could be accomplished between face-to-face meetings if direct lines of communication were present. I agreed, as long as I was apprised of the details of the conversations and no issue was considered agreed upon until Rich and I had discussed it.

Rich recorded in his notes that he told Jeff "the June 8th phone call would not entail negotiations, as I could not agree to any terms at this time, but would help each party understand the position of the other." While the two might not have officially agreed on any one term, they did advance the cause by fleshing out the outstanding issues. This was essential for any future meetings to be productive because we needed a roadmap in front of us to guide us to our ultimate destination: a new lease.

The map Rich and Jeff put together was a long one, with many twists and turns. Rich's original proposed "issues list" was two pages of general bullet points. Now, however, it was a five-and-a-half-page outline of general topics and many subtopics. While the list was too long to describe in detail here, it examined all major facets of the transaction, from the ground rules of the negotiation, to the length of term, capital improvements, operating assistance, and non-relocation agreement, to smaller items like stadium-naming rights, concessions, parking revenues, the Toronto series, and even items such as the income tax implications of where games were held for New York State taxation purposes. The Bills and the County knew that while the State might not be an active participant to this point, it eventually would be, and all of these terms would have to be addressed.

One major change was proposed to the ground rules of negotiation: while the County wanted the end lease to be "comparable to other deals of similar type recently negotiated, recognizing that no two deals are alike," Jeff wanted to change this to the "deal should be fair in comparison to other recently negotiated NFL deals taking into account the scope of investment and revenue opportunities in the club's home market." While the change might appear subtle, it was in fact quite significant. In effect, Jeff was saying that one cannot compare recent NFL stadium deals on an "apples-to-apples" basis but must look at the underlying economics of each market.

We interpreted this to be the team's way of saying, "because Buffalo is a small market with less revenue opportunities than Dallas, New York, or San Francisco, the government must contribute a greater percentage of the final cost for any new infrastructure compared to larger market deals because we cannot generate enough in revenues to pay for our added expense." While I did not necessarily agree with the premise of the Bills' argument, it at least told us what they were thinking and how they viewed themselves in comparison to other teams.

After receiving and reviewing the updated list over the weekend (June 9 was a Saturday), Rich and I talked about the phone conversation on Monday, June 12, and he noted how Jeff's frustration came through every time a topic was discussed that would inevitably require State participation. He also noted how, once they started to talk, both started to fall back into their roles from fifteen years earlier—negotiators, quasi-partners, and people frustrated with State administration. While I would not call Rich and Jeff good friends, they definitely developed a level of trust over the years and it helped to overcome issues that existed and were yet to develop.

The new issues list also became the agenda for the next meeting, now scheduled for June 18, 2012, once again at my office's conference room. As had been the norm between the parties, the agenda was shared with all prior to the meetings. While there were no surprises for the Bills' and County's negotiating teams, I am fairly sure the expanded agenda did take Sam Hoyt and Steve Gawlik by surprise (not least because Sam had told me so before the meeting). I told him the County and Bills were in constant talks and would continue to move the process forward even if the State did not.

Based on my prior discussions with Joe Percoco and Sam, while I was hopeful someone else from the State would attend the June 18 meeting with Sam and Steve, what I really wanted to see was a changed position from Sam and Steve indicating they were given authority to negotiate on behalf of the State. When I walked into the meeting, only Sam and Steve were present for the State, and as the meeting progressed I realized the more things changed, the more they remained the same: they still had no authority to agree to a term.

The County's and Bills' attendees to the meeting were generally the same. Rich Tobe, Liz Burakowski, Mike Siragusa, and I represented the County, along with Chris Melvin and Martha Anderson from Nixon Peabody LLP. Jeff Littmann, Russ Brandon, Mary Owen, Mike Schiavone, and Eugene Driker represented the Bills.

Though I had met Eugene Driker at the May 29 meeting, I could not remember his name during the current meeting. As a result, I inelegantly identified Mr. Driker as "Old Geezer" in my notes for the meeting. I do not remember Gene saying much, if anything, during the meeting that merited a response from me. My meeting notes do not identify him as saying anything, which was probably all well and good; otherwise, I may have been left to say, "to counter the Old Geezer's point . . ." Thankfully that did not occur.

What did occur was a very comprehensive presentation by Jeff on even more points about the NFL's G4 program than he had discussed before. Jeff handed out an NFL document entitled "G4 Stadium Financing Program Selected Financing Guidelines," dated June 14, 2012. While not long, the document shed light on what the NFL expected for a team to participate in the program, with three essential elements. First, the project must pass an "Incremental Revenue Rule Test" in which the new revenue generated by the project showed an increase for a fifteen-year period, based on a league-wide impact, not just the team. Second, each project must meet specific debt guidelines pertaining to total debt of the team and its debt service payments. Third, the project's timetable must not exceed thirty months. Ominously, the NFL document ended with the following: "Meeting these guidelines does not assure approval, as the project is reviewed comprehensively by the League/member clubs."

To meet the three main G4 terms, my notes indicate Jeff said the team would have to remain "in compliance through the fifteen-year amortization period, to be paid out of visiting share of club seat premiums and the nonvisiting share of gate receipts." In response to our question as to how much was possibly available under the G4 program for the project, Jeff stated that he would not state how much was available "as we needed to resolve the other issues before they commit to a certain dollar figure."

I took his response to indicate not that he didn't know, but that he would not state how much until we agreed on other issues such as the scope of the project and term. He did note that if the G4 program was unavailable to them, they could still use the older G3 program, but that offered less NFL assistance (34 percent compared to 50 percent). Both programs required the full amount to be paid back to the NFL upon the sale of a team. This would be a problem for the team because of Mr. Wilson's age and the distinct possibility he might die before the end of the new lease's term. Russ and Jeff both noted that while the problem existed, the team was committed to participating in either of the programs and finding a way to figure out the due-on-sale terms with the NFL in the future if need be.

The discussion then moved to the topic near and dear to me: the term of the lease and the need for a non-relocation agreement. Similar to the last meeting, Jeff noted that the team was "fully prepared to repay the taxpayer money invested in the project if they cannot commit to the full term." He noted if the final agreed-on stadium renovation project was for the full $220 million project they were seeking, the team would agree to accept a ten-year term with the debt service terms based off of a fifteen-year repayment amortization and lease schedule. He also stated the team would not commit to a non-relocation agreement but would repay the governments' investment based off of an amortized buyout, similar to the 1998 lease's provisions.

This was unacceptable to me. I noted while we might be amenable to a fifteen-year lease, we would require a non-relocation agreement and there could be no buyout provision, as there had been in the 1998 lease. I would not commit to investing tens of millions of taxpayer dollars toward a renovation project and then see the team, potentially under a new owner, pay just two or three million dollars and leave, as the 1998 lease provided. Rich noted there was no way we could commit to a $220 million project and watch the team leave in just a few years.

Considering the team agreed to accept a ten-year lease under a fifteen-year amortization schedule, I figured they might accept a fifteen-year term in the long run (they had already admitted they planned on spreading debt service payments over a fifteen-year term) if we committed to the $220 million project. But at this point the term was less of an issue than getting an ironclad non-relocation agreement. If we could not get a non-relocation agreement signed by the team, it put the community in a far worse position in the event Mr. Wilson passed away and a new owner subsequently tried to move the team.

Having practiced bankruptcy law as an attorney, I knew there was a major difference between a lease for real property and an agreement to perform a specific task. A lease can be easily terminated in a bankruptcy proceeding; a non-relocation agreement is a totally different type of agreement in the eyes of the law because it requires specific performance by a party and is much more difficult to terminate. We needed a separate non-relocation agreement regardless of the length of term because it was the strongest legal mechanism we could rely on to guarantee the team stayed here upon the sale of the team to a new owner. While we trusted Mr. Wilson to not move the team prior to his death, we certainly could not trust a party we did not know.

It was clear we would not be resolving the term of lease or the need for a non-relocation agreement at this meeting. With the County and Bills at different positions, and the State once again not participating to any real degree, reaching a mutual agreement would have to wait for another day. As much of the time set aside for the meeting had already been used, we turned to only a few other issues, such as how the project would be spaced out, whether a project labor agreement would be utilized, and how much operational assistance would be provided by the County and State to the team on an annual basis.

As to the length of project, the Bills were seeking the entire $220 million project to be spread out over three years: $35 million of "minor work" to be done in year one; $111 million of major reconstruction work to be completed in year two; and the remaining $74 million allotted to work over the final year. While not agreeing to the full set of projects and the time period, we argued that no matter what size the project turned out to be, a Project Labor Agreement (PLA) with local labor hiring provisions must be entered into by the Bills because (1) the project would be on a public facility and local county law required it; (2) local taxpayers who were helping to pay for the project should also reap some of the bounty of the project by being hired for the construction jobs; and (3) it would avoid any possible union protests that could result in unwanted attention and delays.

Surprisingly, the team had no objections. We expected Mr. Wilson to reject any notion of entering into a PLA, but Jeff Littmann noted that since a high percentage of qualified local contractors for the project would be union contractors, it made sense for a PLA to be in place. I was pleased to get what we thought might be a contentious term off the table early, especially considering we really didn't have to give anything to get it.

Getting back to the length of the project's schedule, either Rich or I (I don't remember, and my notes don't identify who said it) noted the County did not object to a three-year construction time period. In fact, a three-year construction period was preferable for the County because it would allow us to spread any capital borrowings the County completed to pay for our portion of the construction costs over a longer period. The idea of potentially borrowing up to $100 million at once was not palatable; borrowing $33 million a year over a three-year period was acceptable because the County borrowed approximately $30 million on average annually. The only issue to be resolved was that the NFL's G4 program required all construction to be completed in thirty months, not thirty-six. However, this was an issue for the Bills to resolve, not the County, and the Bills said they would work on getting a waiver from the NFL for the thirty-month requirement.

While getting an agreement on a PLA or spreading the construction over a three-year period might not have been huge in the grand scheme of things, it did show that the Bills and the County were willing to agree on terms. Unfortunately, the same could not be said of the State. Neither Sam nor Steve could accept such terms, though they did say they would recommend to the powers that be to agree to them. Considering that the terms we were agreeing on were fairly noncontroversial as they pertained to the State, I believed the State would likely support them.

One area that would be controversial and required the State's participation would be determining the annual operating and game-day capital provided to the Bills by the County and State. The County could not agree to an amount for the State, so it was essential that the State be an active participant in this part of the negotiation. The Bills proposed continuing the same payments with an annual increase based on an inflation index. However, there was no way this could be discussed if neither Sam nor Steve had the authority to bind the State.

And this discussion was important because we were not talking about cents on the dollar. Based on the 1998 lease agreement, the County was to provide the Bills approximately $4.01 million for game-day and operating expenses in the next year, the County was to contribute another $2.99 million for capital expenses at the stadium, and the State was to provide $3 million for additional working capital to the team. In all, the Bills were slated to receive approximately $10 million from the County and State for operating and infrastructure capital.

Our goal on the County's side was to reduce this amount to the lowest level possible, but we could not begin to negotiate in good faith when the State was not an active participant. I certainly would not commit the County to paying any amount until the State and County had agreed on our own respective payments, if any. Thus, while the Bills revealed what they wanted as part of the next deal—a continuation of payments with an annual increase for inflation—no real negotiation could take place until the State became an active player.

After about two and a half hours, we wrapped up the meeting, noting that reaching an agreement on some terms was a good start. However, just like the last meeting, we knew we were not going to get much further toward a final lease until the State entered the negotiations.

Chapter 11

At Least They Fed Us

Leaving the meeting on June 18, 2012, I felt we were taking baby steps toward our ultimate goal. It was time for all parties to ramp-up our meetings and conversations, and that meant everyone—the County, Bills, and New York State. So after the meeting on June 18, all parties agreed to meet again as soon as possible. I was glad the Bills had suggested the stadium as a location for the next meeting, and even happier when we all agreed to hold the meeting on June 29. Now we were definitely moving—well, as fast as you can move when of three participants only two are involved.

Following the prior meeting, Rich and Jeff continued to speak to each other to try to resolve noncontroversial issues, and I was tasked to try to find out what was actually happening on the State level. Unfortunately, no matter who I spoke to, I usually got the same response: Sam and Steve are relaying information back to the powers that be in Albany and New York City, and all would progress in due course.

While we had no assurances the State would become actively involved, the County and the Bills decided to move ahead with the June 29 meeting because we wanted to discuss a number of topics not covered much before, specifically the Bills in Toronto series. The meeting was scheduled for 10 a.m. at the Ralph. Driving into the stadium complex that morning, I felt for the first time during the negotiations that not much would be accomplished today. Negotiations continued to flounder because of the State's lack of involvement. Nevertheless,

I walked into the Bills' administration building with a smile, and we were led into the stadium, as the meeting was to be held in the M&T Bank enclosed club seat sections in the east end-zone side.

Three tables were laid out in a triangle behind the last row of seats in the enclosed box. A nice spread of bagels, pastries, fruit, and other snacks were set up on an adjoining table with waitstaff from Delaware North's concession business at hand to serve our every need. Joining me from the County were Rich Tobe, Mike Siragusa, Liz Burakowski, and outside counsel of Chris Melvin and Martha Anderson. The Bills were represented by Jeff Littmann, Russ Brandon, Mary Owen, Mike Schiavone, and Eugene Driker (who this time I called "Old Guy" in my notes because I again forgot his name). New York State was once again represented by Sam Hoyt and Steve Gawlik.

Before starting discussions, Russ mentioned to me that as part of the requested renovations, the team intended to combine the two enclosed club seat areas, the M&T Bank club and Time Warner Cable club, into one and convert the other into the written and local press box. He said the team was never able to sell out either club facility. In fact, he told me both clubs were only 50 percent occupied. Combining the two into one would thereby create a sold-out club and allow the team to more productively use the other for the press facility. Seeing the enclosed box, with windows that could not be opened, I understood why the team had trouble selling out two sets of these boxes: part of the game-day experience is lost without feeling the wind, snow, or cold on your face and hearing the roar of the crowd unimpeded by glass.

After everyone chose their breakfast, we sat down at the tables. The Bills table was full; the County's table was full; and the State's table . . . well, there were a few open spots there, so Liz and Chris chose to sit with Sam and Steve. Rich passed out an agenda that he and Jeff had agreed to before the meeting. There were now fifteen main headings to the agenda, with many, many subheadings. Certain headings and subheadings were in bold, which signified the items to be discussed at the meeting. After flipping through the agenda, and finishing off my bagel, we got down to the business at hand, which entailed the Bills making formal requests on topics we had not discussed to this point.

Russ opened up the meeting, thanked everyone for attending, and then thanked all for their conscientious effort to move the process along. I took this as a little dig at the State, but one done in a nice manner. He then spoke of how the effort to tap into the Southern Ontario market had been a success for the team, and the key to that effort was the team playing one regular home season game in Toronto.

I expected Russ to say then that the team must play at least one regular season "home" game a year in Toronto. I was willing to agree to that point, but that is not what happened. Russ and Jeff alternated the argument, but it was clear to me and the others at the table that the team had something different in mind: if the NFL should go to an eighteen-game regular season schedule, as had been rumored, the Bills wanted the additional home game to be played in Toronto. In effect, if there were nine home games, instead of the current eight, seven would be played at the Ralph and the other two at Rogers Center in Toronto.

This surprised me. In fact, it angered me, though I did not show it. I thought, "They have a lot of gall asking for more than $200 million of work to be done on the stadium, but if they get an additional home game they want to play it in Canada."

As I stewed in my seat, I started to think of late-night TV commercials: "But wait, there's more!" Jeff said the NFL might assign the Bills to play an international game in London, England, or Mexico City. If so, the team would agree to replace the extra Toronto game with the international game if the regular season was an eighteen-game schedule. However, if the regular season remained at sixteen games, the Bills wanted the right to hold the international game as the host club, hold a home game in Toronto, and then hold six regular-season home games in Buffalo.

I remember Rich Tobe looking my way and, in his expression, imploring me not to blow my top. He could tell I was not happy. I looked at Sam and saw my exasperation mirrored in his face. Rich, the wise sage among us, said in a very diplomatic tone that holding another game in Toronto would be very difficult for us to agree to. I added that the public was demanding us to eliminate the Toronto game presently on the schedule, and adding another game there would be roundly criticized.

Looking back on it now, I'm not sure the Bills really wanted to play another game in Toronto. They might have been using this as a bargaining chip to retain the right to play one regular-season home game in Toronto. Even today, I can't fathom that the Bills expected us to give in and let them play an additional game in Toronto. I'm sure they would have reaped a significant financial reward by playing a second game in Canada, but there was no way we were going to agree to the idea.

I think the Bills' negotiating team could see this was a nonstarter for the County, so Jeff immediately moved on to the next major item on the agenda: an update on the NFL's response to the team's G4 financing request. Jeff noted the NFL had not provided its final report to the team, but it "looks likely we qualify for a G4 loan." He went through many of the conditions precedent to receiving league approval (return on investment test, thirty-month completion rule), and it appeared all would be met. However, Jeff added a proviso that put a damper on his initial analysis: there would in all likelihood "be no benefit to the Bills because of the due-on-sale clause."

In effect, Jeff was saying that while the proposed project would qualify under the G4 loan program, the possibility of having to sell the team after Mr. Wilson's death during the loan repayment term meant the entire loan would have to be repaid immediately upon sale, making the loan program less valuable for the current ownership. If the G4 program was of no real benefit to the team, it was likely the team would try to limit its capital contribution to the stadium's renovation. About this time I started thinking, "this meeting is becoming a total disaster."

But wait! Again, there was more. Jeff then mentioned the phrase we had not heard from team representatives and thought was a dead topic—personal seat licenses (PSLs). He launched into an analysis of the way other recent stadium deals were structured—that is, the percentage paid for by the public and the percentage paid for with private money. For example, he noted that in the construction of Pittsburgh's Heinz Field, $176 million came from public entities and $76 million from private dollars, with $30 million covered by PSLs; in Cincinnati, the private contribution was 6 percent and covered by "chartered seat licenses;" in Cleveland, the private contribution was approximately 25 percent of the stadium's cost, entirely covered by PSLs; and so on and so on.

Jeff did mention that there were circumstances over the past twenty years in which PSLs were not used, such as Baltimore in 1998 and Jacksonville in 1995. However, it was clear from his listing of more than twelve recent stadium deals, with the vast majority of them including PSLs, that he was putting them on the table, especially if the team did not take advantage of the G4 loan program.

The Bills team then distributed a number of spreadsheets titled "Ralph Wilson Stadium Key Economic Lease Terms," with different subheadings, including "Lease Term and Termination Rights," "Annual New York State Working Capital Investment," and "Annual Erie County Investment." Looking at these spreadsheets, I could see the meeting was not going to get any better.

The first sheet, "Lease Term and Termination Rights," had two main columns "1998 Lease" and "Proposed Extension." To the left of the columns were a number of row headings that ran the gamut from "Age of Stadium" at beginning of lease term to "Non-Relocation Period" to "Base Buyout Fee." The rows under "1998 Lease" were all filled with the terms of the then current lease, and the rows under "Proposed Extension" were all blank. It was thus clear to me that the Bills' team were going to reveal their "ask" for each, at least beyond what we already knew.

They then began going through each major point. On the term of the lease, they held firm to ten years, and reiterated they would not seek a contingency period like in the old lease. Nothing Jeff or Russ said at this time surprised any of us, as they had already discussed these points. When it came down to the right to terminate, they did say something that surprised us: they wanted the right to terminate immediately at any time during the new lease's term. We knew the team wanted to keep in the lease agreement the right to move upon sale, but we assumed there would be a locked-in period similar to the 1998 lease in which the team could not terminate the lease and relocate until at least the sixth year of the lease agreement.

Now the team was telling us they wanted the right to terminate the new lease immediately, even if future renovations had not been completed. All I could imagine was Mr. Wilson dying in the first year of the new lease, the team being sold to an out-of-town owner, and then being moved prior to the next season. Meanwhile, we would have a partially renovated white elephant sitting in Orchard Park. I looked at Rich Tobe, and now he looked exasperated. I just bit my tongue, determined to listen to the rest of the Bills' negotiating team's presentation.

Jeff did note, as he had said before, the team was willing to repay an amortized amount of the State and County's investment in the new lease if the team did move. "Mr. Wilson was committed to ensuring the public entities' investment is repaid if the team should move," was how he put it. The reference to an "amortized amount" told me the team would pay back a portion of the governments' investment depending on when the relocation took place. So in year one we would get repaid pretty much the whole investment, but not in year two, and so on.

By this time, they were passing out cookies to each of the tables. I think I grabbed four or five and started munching away, as much out of stress as from a sweet tooth. I figured I might as well get as much to eat for free from the Bills considering it was doubtful we would get a lease done under these terms. We were asked if we had any questions regarding the team's requested terms. I'm sure I said, "No."

Next, the team moved on to the spreadsheet subtitled "Annual New York State Working Capital Investment." This spreadsheet revealed some interesting statistics. The team noted the "NFL Average Net Ticket Revenue" in 2011 was $49,209,836 and the "Buffalo Bills Net Ticket Revenue" the same year was $35,261,934—a nearly $14 million shortfall. Noted on the spreadsheet was the State's annual contribution to the team. Unknown to many in the public, throughout the 1998 lease, New York State provided the Bills with an annual working capital grant of $3 million. Now on this spreadsheet, the team was seeking an increase to $4,730,725 with a corresponding annual percentage increase.

Looking at Sam Hoyt and Steve Gawlik, I could see them writing down notes on the sheet. They had little to say. In that regard not much had changed from prior meetings, even though this was a topic that directly affected the State.

With not much discussion from Sam and Steve, the Bills then moved to the next page—"Annual Erie County Investment." This spreadsheet was much more detailed, primarily because the County had provided the Bills millions of dollars annually combined under three areas: "Game-Day Expenses," "Operating Expenses," and a "Capital Improvement Allowance." Under the last year of the 1998 lease, the County paid a combined $7,111,423 to the Bills for these three areas. After Jeff explained 'the various reasons an increase was warranted, reasons I did not agree with, it became pretty evident the team was seeking a significant increase in subsidy from the County: $350,000 each for the game-day and operating expense accounts and an additional $1.6 million for the annual capital improvement for required stadium maintenance. In the end, the annual $7.1 million subsidy the County made to the Bills would increase to $9,291,541, with annual increases thereafter. This amount was in addition to any contribution the County would make for the proposed renovations.

It was about then that I looked around for a Delaware North representative to find a beer for me. I needed a drink. Unfortunately, no rep was around.

I didn't say much during their presentation, as I understood this to be the team's opportunity to present its views on key terms. If I had spoken, I likely would have lost my cool. I have learned over many negotiations that just because an opposing party asks for a certain term, they don't expect to get it. I kept quiet and thought that if I were in their place I would probably have asked for the same terms.

We discussed a few of the Bills' assumptions apparent in their financial spreadsheets and touched on some other terms, but by then all parties were tired—the Bills from making their presentation, and the County and State's teams from having to hear these "requests." We agreed the next meeting would be on July 15 or 16 at a location to be determined, and then we all shook hands. I don't recall anyone claiming the meeting had been productive.

Heading back to the Rath Building, Rich, Liz, and I discussed our individual takeaways from the meeting. We all came to the same conclusion—getting a lease done would be extremely difficult if the team held to their terms as described, especially their right to terminate the lease at any time.

"There's not much positive to say about that meeting," I remarked. "But at least they fed us."

Chapter 12

The Letter

In any negotiation, there are times when you feel you're at a critical juncture. We had reached that point. It was time to get down to hardcore negotiations of terms. The Bills and the County had pretty much revealed their respective asks to the others as pertaining to a new lease. What was missing was the participation of New York State.

During the preceding few weeks, I had spoken to many members of the Cuomo administration, warning that negotiations would soon stall if the State did not get fully involved. I consistently received the same response: the governor and his administration were being kept up to date on the negotiations. At various times, I had spoken to the governor, lieutenant governor, and high-level assistants. I had no reason to believe Sam and Steve were not passing the information up the chain of command. In fact, Sam had told me that he talked to the governor after each of our meetings. I concluded that the higher-ups were not taking the discussions seriously.

With the next meeting coming up in about two weeks, Rich and I agreed it was time to put in writing our concerns about the State's inaction. We agreed that I would not sign the letter, and that the letter would not go directly to Governor Cuomo, as doing either might sour our relations. Instead, we would send a letter to a high-ranking official in the administration. We informed Sam of our intentions. I don't think he was thrilled with the idea, but he knew it was necessary.

So on July 5, 2012, Rich Tobe sent Kenneth Adams, the president and CEO of the Empire State Development Corporation (ESD), a letter describing the status of the lease negotiations. Rich sent the letter via postal mail and email. We had decided to address the letter to Adams for three reasons: (1) the Erie County Stadium Corporation, which was the current lessee of the stadium, was a division of ESD; (2) Adams was technically Sam's boss, though Sam really worked for the governor; and (3) Rich had developed a rapport with Ken regarding economic development projects we were working on together. Copies of the letter were sent also to Sam and to Leecia Eve, Deputy Secretary for Economic Affairs for the Cuomo Administration, an old friend of Rich's and mine who just happened to be a Buffalo native who had the ear of the governor.

Rather than summarize the letter, I include it here in full because I think it reflects what we felt was necessary to get the State's full attention.

July 5, 2012

Mr. Kenneth Adams
President and CEO
Empire State Development Corporation
633 Third Avenue, 37th Floor
New York, New York 10017

Dear Ken,

As you know, we have been meeting with the Buffalo Bills for several months to discuss the terms of a lease extension between the Buffalo Bills and Erie County, the Erie County Stadium Corporation (a subsidiary of Empire State Development Corporation) and New York State.

All meetings have been conducted in Erie County, either at the Rath County Office Building or at Ralph Wilson Stadium, and all sessions have included Sam Hoyt and Steve Gawlik representing New York State. At our last meeting, on June 29, the Bills finished their presentations and clearly stated what they are seeking. Although we believe there is room to negotiate, we are now nearing the point where the State and County must reply indicating our positions.

As you know, the State representatives have not been in a position to provide the State's position on the Bills' proposals, and we chose not to do so in order that we have a common position with the State. While I expect and hope that the State and County will be on the same page with regard to some important matters such as lease term, non-relocation agreement, M/WBE, PLA, blackout provisions, etc., we must each indicate the extent to which we can provide financial assistance to stadium renovation projects and to the franchise.

In order for us to reply to the Bills, it is imperative that the State and County have discussions that can lead to a proposal to the Bills and that we do so now in order to make such a response to the Bills later this month.

While we expect that the County will make a significant contribution to the project as we did sixteen years ago, we are now faced with very severe financial constraints that did not exist at the time of the last lease. These constraints limit our ability to meet the Bills' requests. We hope and expect that acting together we will be able to place the Bills a responsible and affordable offer that will induce them to remain in Erie County and to meet our mutual goals of a competitive, financially stable team for many years to come.

We therefore request that meetings take place between the State and County that will lead to the development of a joint position. We are prepared to meet at your convenience here in Buffalo or in New York City or in Albany.

Our next meeting with the Bills is scheduled for July 16. Please be advised that County Executive Poloncarz will be in New York City on July 11 and 12 attending meetings with ratings agencies during the afternoon of the 11th and morning of the 12th. If you are available either the evening of the 11th or the afternoon of the 12th, he and I would be delighted to discuss the matter with you further. It is important these meetings take place as soon as possible as we have a great deal of ground to cover before the next scheduled meeting with the Bills on July 16.

We intend to review with the Bills the state of County finances at that meeting. Considering the parties have met numerous times over the past few months, we should present an offer to the Bills at the end of that meeting. While the County is ready to discuss the matter further, unless the State is ready to do the same it is doubtful that any progress will be made at said meeting. Therefore, it is incumbent on the State to be prepared to make an offer to the Bills in conjunction with the County. If not, negotiations will need to be put on hold until such time as the State is ready, which would defeat the goals of all involved to reach an agreement on the basic terms before the start of the National Football League's training camp in mid-August and execution of a final agreement by the end of 2012.

We look forward to hearing from you and to meeting with you in the near future.

Sincerely yours,

Richard Tobe,
Deputy County Executive

I knew the letter would increase the chance of the State becoming more involved, but it might also backfire. The State might look at the letter as an attempt by the County to "throw the State under the bus" in the event talks ceased or, worst-case scenario, Mr. Wilson died before we could hammer out an agreement. In effect, it was both. We needed the State to be more actively involved, and if things did go bad I was not going to publicly wear the crown of blame for losing the Bills. We had worked our tails off to that point, and now it was time for the State to do the same.

Knowing the Cuomo administration as well as we did, Rich and I expected a fairly immediate response, and we received one—though not a very helpful one. Rich received a call from Ken Adams soon after he received the letter, and I heard from Joe Percoco. This let us know the governor knew of the letter's existence.

We were both told things would be ratcheted up and that the State would play a much greater role in the coming weeks. Leecia Eve told me the same thing a few days later when I saw her at a local event. I didn't perceive any anger as a result of the letter, though I don't think the administration appreciated us putting on record their inaction. If local media had presented us with a Freedom of Information Law request for any communication between the County and State pertaining to the Bills lease, the letter would inevitably have to be released, thereby revealing to the public that the talks had reached a standstill and the State was to blame. If that were to occur, we knew the administration would be furious with us, and the governor furious with me, but it was a risk worth taking to move the State along.

What we did not receive from the State was an agreement to meet with a County official to discuss our next steps. This bothered me because if the State could not find the time to meet with us and move forward after we sent the letter, it was doubtful the next meeting could be held. It also meant the possibility of moving forward anytime soon would be jeopardized, as once training camp began, the Bills would be preoccupied with that instead of the negotiations.

Calls went back and forth between County and State officials, but not much could be agreed upon. So on July 12, 2012, Rich Tobe was part of a conference call with Sam Hoyt and other State officials during which it was officially decided to postpone the meeting scheduled for July 16, 2012. The task of informing the Bills was left to Rich, who called Jeff Littmann with the news and sent a confirming email afterward. The following day, Rich sent Sam an email, copying me on it, stating the following:

Sam,

As we discussed last night, we have decided to postpone the three-way meeting scheduled with the Buffalo Bills for Monday July 16.

As you know, the Bills have completed making their request to us and are expecting a response. We cannot provide such a response until the County and State have had discussions and develop a joint reply. Unfortunately, we have not been able to engage in substantive talks with the State yet.

We have been analyzing the Bills' request and are prepared to share the results with the State as a first step in seeking to develop a common position. Please let us know when we can meet with you and the other state officials who will be involved in this matter. As we mentioned when we requested the meeting for earlier this week, we are prepared to travel to Albany or New York City or to host meetings here in Buffalo.

We look forward to hearing from you.

Rich

We were in a stalemate. There was not much we could do other than go public with the information, which would have destroyed our relationship with the State.

We had heard through the grapevine that some senior advisors to the governor had advised him to go very slow on the lease negotiations because the 1998 Lease did not expire until after completion of the 2012 football season—technically, not until the middle of 2013—so there was no real reason to rush. If this was the case, the governor was receiving poor advice. Mr. Wilson, now in his early nineties, could pass any day, which would put the future of the franchise in Buffalo in jeopardy. I knew from talking to the governor on numerous occasions that he understood the importance the community placed on the Bills, so I could not understand why his administration would risk losing the team.

By now I was quite worried that a new lease would not be agreed upon and signed before Mr. Wilson passed away. This meant Buffalo might lose their beloved Bills.

Chapter 13

Thank God We Got Schumed!

Following the decision to postpone the July 16 meeting, Rich Tobe and Jeff Littmann kept up a steady stream of emails and occasional phone calls during the following days, though for all intents and purposes we were stuck in a stalemate of the State's doing. On August 1, Rich and Jeff spoke by telephone, generally lamenting the failure of the State to move forward but also attempting to resolve some basic issues the County had with the Bills' determination of future costs as revealed at the past meeting.

During the call, Jeff told Rich that the team had spoken to Senator Charles ("Chuck") Schumer about the issues related to the G4 program's "due-on-sale" clause as it impacted the Bills. Jeff told Rich he expected the senator to speak very soon to NFL Commissioner Roger Goodell and other high-level NFL officials about finding a way to solve the problem. According to Rich's notes of the meeting (he emailed them to Liz Burakowski, Mike Siragusa, and me), Jeff did not advise Senator Schumer of the problems the team and County were encountering with the State. However, the commissioner was aware of the issue, and there was a good chance he would pass that information on to the senator. Rich advised me to expect a call from the senator soon.

Politics is a funny business. Elected officials may be from the same political party but that does not mean they are the best of friends. You learn to navigate the waters of politics and governing knowing full well there are many captains in many boats, some boats bigger than others.

One such relationship was that between Governor Andrew Cuomo and Senator Chuck Schumer. Governor Cuomo and Senator Schumer had worked together on many occasions for the betterment of the people of New York State. They were (and are) both strong personalities, however, and did not always agree on the best course to take.

Among political circles, Senator Schumer is known for his press conferences in which he comes into a community to speak on a particular issue regardless of what might otherwise be happening that day in the community. Often, the senator will fly in, hold a press conference on a subject matter, and then fly away, stealing any media coverage from others for the day. In political circles, these press conferences have come to be known as being "Schumed." If you got Schumed, that meant you had an event scheduled for the same time as one of the senator's press conferences, and he stole all the media coverage, and perhaps your thunder. We have all been Schumed at least once in our careers.

So, on August 7, I was not surprised to hear from my secretary that Senator Schumer was on the phone wishing to speak to me about a press conference he was planning to hold the next day in Buffalo. Taking the call, I exchanged pleasantries with the senator, and then he got down to business.

Senator Schumer explained he would be holding a press conference the next day in front of Ralph Wilson Stadium to announce "a major new proposal which will help keep the Bills in Buffalo." For the next few minutes we discussed issues relating to the NFL's G4 program's "due-on-sale" clause as it related to the Bills renovations and future sale. Knowing all about the G4 program, I thanked him for any efforts he could make to change the program to make it more beneficial for use in Buffalo.

He noted he had spoken to the commissioner about the matter, and he thought the NFL was receptive to his proposed amendments to the due-on-sale clause of the G4 program. He told me his proposed changes would "guarantee the team stays in Buffalo," and he would announce as much the following morning at the press conference.

I thanked him for his efforts and said any change in the "due-on-sale" clause could only positively impact the chances of keeping the team in Buffalo. However, I warned him that the media would swamp him with questions on the current status of negotiations and how the proposed change would actually help, especially if he said it would guarantee the team stays. I told him how all parties had agreed not to discuss the status of lease talks, and the media was desperate for any morsel of information they could obtain. Then I mentioned the stalemate in talks and how we couldn't do anything until the State became an active participant. I went into detail on the number of meetings we had held over the past few months and how everything was in the State's hands at this point. He was quiet for a second, and then he said he had "heard something like that from Roger Goodell." He thought his press conference would help move the State along.

He thanked me for my advice on being prepared to face a desperate media looking for any information on the lease talks and told me he expected he would "be able to control the narrative." I wished him well and said we should talk after the press conference.

I have been a party to many of Senator Schumer's press conferences over the years. He has always impressed me with his ability to handle the press. However, when I heard his August 8 press conference being live-streamed by the local sports radio station's website, it was quite evident he had no control over the conference. Media members were like rabid dogs ripping at the flesh of some poor, defenseless animal. The media did not understand the G4 financing program or how it could help keep the Bills in Buffalo. This did not surprise me because no one from the bargaining teams had ever discussed the G4 program with the media. To them the senator's declaration of a guarantee to save the team made no sense.

I winced every time a media member attacked the senator for not giving any information out about the current lease talks and discussing instead some obscure financing program that no one understood. The senator was in fact trying to show he was helping, but as it sounded on the radio, the media did not understand and thought he was grandstanding.

What the senator did not realize at that moment was that his press conference was having a huge effect. The State was now fully engaged in what was occurring at the Ralph. Actually, make that "enraged": Senator Schumer was stealing everyone else's thunder. When State officials heard of the senator's plans to hold a press conference at the Ralph to announce a "major new proposal" to save the team, it seemed like every

State official wanted to get involved. Rich Tobe received a number of phone calls and emails from Sam Hoyt, Ken Adams, and Leecia Eve inquiring into what the senator would say. I received calls from various staff members, including my longtime friend John Maggiore, who was chief of staff to Lieutenant Governor Robert Duffy, trying to find out what the senator was up to.

Regardless of whether the senator's press conference was a success in the media and public's eyes, it was an unconditional success for me. His conference lit a fire under the State, a fire where not even a spark had been before. In no time, not only were our calls returned, but the governor's office started to actually *do* things. I looked over at Jennifer Hibit, my chief of staff, and said, "For the first and probably only time in my life I will say this: Thank God we got Schumed!"

Almost immediately after the press conference ended, my secretary said Senator Schumer was on the phone. Calling me from his car, he asked me if I had heard the press conference. I responded that I had and that the media had been even worse than I anticipated. He responded, "You were right. The media continually asked about current lease talks" and whether or not his holding the press conference meant the talks were falling apart.

He told me he hadn't thought "it would be as wild as it was" and that it was clear the "media did not understand the G4 program." I confirmed that we had never discussed the program with the media, nor discussed with them any facet of the status of negotiations. Unfortunately, because we never discussed lease status, and he was the first major official to talk about lease issues, he became the lamb being led to slaughter, so to speak. As he said, "All they want is confirmation of any bit of information about the lease negotiations."

He sounded dejected, which is very unusual for the senator. But when I told him the governor's office wanted to know about every bit of his press conference, his spirits picked up. When I mentioned that the governor's office finally seemed engaged, he became ebullient, back to the Chuck Schumer we had all come to know. I thanked him for kicking things into gear and told him I would keep him apprised of lease developments.

About the same time I hung up the phone, Rich Tobe walked into my office and informed me Leecia Eve had called him to say the governor had made a "major announcement" of his own regarding the lease by hiring Irwin Raij, a noted sports law expert and partner at the nationally noted law firm of Foley and Lardner LLP, to advise the State during negotiations.

I went to my computer and typed in Raij's name and immediately saw a news report from ESPN.com in which Governor Cuomo was quoted as saying, "New York state is committed to doing all we can to keep the Bills a part of the Buffalo community, while also protecting taxpayer dollars and seeing that the team can thrive in western New York for years to come."

I told Rich, "The stalemate is over. It won't surprise me if things pick up tremendously." It had taken much longer than it should have, but the State was finally engaged. Perhaps the governor was trying to "out-Schum" Senator Schumer by stealing his thunder with his own announcement. But I didn't care why the governor acted, only that he had. Finally, the State was going to be an active participant in the negotiations.

Thank God we got Schumed.

Chapter 14

It's Pronounced Like the Bread

Following the announcement of Irwin Raij's retention by the State, Rich and I discussed the implications for lease negotiations. We had always assumed the governor would entrust a high-level official in his administration to act as the State's main negotiator. We were not sure at the time if the hiring of Mr. Raij would change that, with Raij taking over the State's negotiations, or if he would act solely as a consultant.

I wanted to learn more about Raij, and the best place to learn about anyone is, of course, the Internet. I immediately found out a lot about him. Foley and Lardner's site described Irwin Raij as a partner of the firm and co-chair of its "Sports Industry Team," whatever that meant, as well as practicing in the areas of government, real estate, and finance law. Having practiced myself in those areas, I started to feel more comfortable with Raij's hiring. Just as you wouldn't hire a criminal attorney to close a billion-dollar corporate takeover, you wouldn't hire a corporate attorney to try a major criminal case. It was important the State hired an attorney who knew the intricacies of sports law, as well as the ancillary areas that are part of it.

It became clear to me that Raij would bring a significant knowledge of professional sports and its management to the discussion. According to his bio, he had led the group, including Magic Johnson, that had recently purchased the Los Angeles Dodgers (my favorite baseball team, incidentally). He had also been appointed by Major League Baseball commissioner Bud Selig to a three-person panel to determine the feasibility of developing a new stadium for the Oakland A's, and he was MLB's counsel during the Florida Marlins new stadium talks and during the relocation of the Montreal Expos to Washington, DC. On top of all this, he had represented Nolan Ryan's group in the purchase of the Texas Rangers and had provided legal and strategic counsel to the Miami Dolphins during the recent improvements made to Sunlife Stadium.

Scrolling down further, I noted that Raij worked on the Al Gore/ Joe Lieberman campaign in a high-level counsel role after previously working in the White House Office of Counsel to the President during the Clinton years. Seeing this made me smile, as not only was Raij a noted expert in the area of sports law, he was most certainly a Democrat, which further bolstered my opinion of him. Still scrolling, I discovered a description of a past job that caught my eye: Raij had begun his career "as an attorney advisor for the [United States] Department of Housing & Urban Development, and returned to the Department to serve as special assistant in the office of general counsel and as acting managing attorney for the FOIA Department."

At that moment I think I said out loud "Bingo!" Here was the connection to Governor Cuomo that I figured had to exist. Prior to running for governor in 2002, Andrew Cuomo had served first as an appointed Assistant Secretary for the Department of Housing & Urban Development (HUD) from 1993 to 1997 and then the Secretary of HUD, all under President Bill Clinton. I figured that Raij and the governor must have worked with each other at HUD during the Clinton years, and that they might even be close friends.

The governor is known for having brilliant individuals working for him, but also for trusting only a few of his staff to accomplish important missions. Joe Percoco, State Director of Operations Howard Glaser, and Secretary to the Governor Larry Schwartz were generally known as his go-to guys depending on the situation. Considering the negotiation of a lease with a professional football team is not considered normal governmental fare, it did not surprise me the governor would retain an outside attorney/consultant to advise him during the course of action. I just did not know to what extent that person would be an advisor or a chief negotiator for the governor. While I still did not have the answer, my theory that the governor and Raij knew each other made it all the more likely that Raij would play a key role in future negotiations, and moreover be someone the governor trusted.

Knowing this was important because while Raij would certainly be working with my team to secure a favorable deal with the Bills, he was not in fact part of my team, but would have the ear of the governor. It was important to Rich and I that we talk with him as soon as possible, both to bring him up to speed with the current status of negotiations, and also to see if we could glean any information from him on what the governor was thinking.

Luckily for us, within a day or two of his hiring, Raij and Rich spoke by phone. He told Rich he would be up in Buffalo in the upcoming week and wanted to meet to discuss the negotiations. On August 14, Rich said, he would be meeting with all of the parties to the talks as part of a "listening tour" as well as an actual tour of Ralph Wilson Stadium.

I asked Rich how Raij pronounced his last name. Rich confessed he wasn't certain, even after the call. We thought it might be "Ra-eye-ch," but we were only guessing. I told Rich he had better just say "Hi Irwin" when he met him and hope he pronounced his last name.

Rich, Liz Burakowski, and I discussed how much information we should share with Irwin. While it was important to close a deal, we had to close it in a way that did not break the County's bank, so to speak. Without much debate, we decided to share everything we knew at that point about the discussions. Because Rich was having more detailed conversations with Jeff Littmann, we assumed that we knew more about the current status of talks than the other State representatives did. Revealing this information to Irwin would be our way of saying he could trust us, and that we assumed he would play an integral role in the talks. Rich asked Liz to update a spreadsheet we had previously made that listed the total amount paid by each party under the then current lease, and we agreed to give this to Irwin when he went on his listening tour.

We also discussed quantifying the financial impact going forward to all parties if the State and County just gave in to the Bills' demands and provided them everything they asked as part of the proposed renovation. This spreadsheet would include not only the proposed renovation price tag, but a continuation of County game-day and operating expenses, annual County capital infrastructure investment, and the State's annual working capital. We would decide whether to give this to Irwin once we saw it.

Finally, we decided to try to determine how much the State would receive in income tax from the Bills organization, its players, coaches, and other employees, as an incentive to show the State how much it would lose in revenue if the team left. Liz agreed to work with the team in our budget office to compile these spreadsheets and get back to Rich and me before Rich met with Irwin on August 14.

On Monday, August 13, 2012, Liz met with Rich and me to go over the spreadsheets. The first spreadsheet, the description of the then current cost under the 1998 lease, showed the State's total payment during the life of the lease to be $122,927,000, and the County had paid out $91,399,000. In total, the County and State investment in the stadium and annual payments to the Bills equaled $214,326,000, with the County paying 42.64 percent and the State 57.36 percent.

It was important to know these figures, as it was my hope the breakdown in costs between the State and County would be roughly similar: 60 percent of the cost borne by the State, and 40 percent by the County. Now that we had someone to negotiate with from the State, we could formally present this ask to the State representatives.

The second spreadsheet, the potential future costs, certainly would get the attention of anyone who read it. In the 1998 lease, the State paid for all the costs of construction, and then the State and County shared future expenses, with the County picking up the greater share. So, in preparing this spreadsheet, Liz and Budget Director Bob Keating listed all renovation expenses in the State's column, gave a larger proportion of future costs to the County, and spread out the total payments over fifteen years (the duration we were seeking as the term of the lease).

If the State and County just caved and gave the Bills what they wanted, over a fifteen-year period, the total cost would be $481,960,000, with the State paying $309,993,000 and the County $171,964,000. This meant the State would pay 64 percent of the cost and the County 36 percent. While we never expected to end up at this total amount, it needed to be quantified so Irwin understood what the Bills were actually seeking from the governments.

It would not be an understatement to say this spreadsheet was eye-popping. There was no way either the County or the State would agree to pay a half-billion dollars to renovate the stadium and contribute to the cost of future operating expenses. If we were to give in to what the Bills requested, the County alone would have paid out $9.3 million in 2013, with that amount eventually growing to $13.9 million in 2027. With all of the needs in our community—from libraries and parks, to road repair, to child protective services and cultural organizations—I could not in good conscience commit that much in annual costs to what was in effect a private business. It might be "our" football team in our community's psyche, but it was first and foremost a business, and no business should be paid out that much annually. With such an incredible figure written on it, there was no question we would be providing the page to Irwin so he understood how much the Bills were seeking.

Finally, Liz and the Budget staff determined the State would receive approximately $210,420,000 over a fifteen-year period from the Bills and its employees in income and other taxes: $120 million from player salaries; $24 million from nonplayer salaries, and an additional $24 million in annual taxable benefits to the State. It was important to provide this spreadsheet to Irwin to show him what the State would lose in revenue if the team should move, and also to get them to realize if they did pay $309,993,000, as indicated on the prior spreadsheet, the State's true out-of-pocket expense over fifteen years would really be about $100 million. That's a drop in the bucket for the State over fifteen years.

Armed with this information, Rich met Irwin on August 14. Rich told me afterward that the meeting was very cordial, with Irwin reiterating that the meeting was part of his "listening tour." Irwin told Rich he had just finished a tour of the stadium and had met with Jeff Littmann for some time to discuss the talks. He noted after his meeting with Rich that he was going to meet with Sam Hoyt and Steve Gawlik to get their impression of the negotiations.

Irwin informed Rich he had been asked by the governor to make recommendations on the best way to proceed going forward. Rich went through the terms of the current lease and of the Bills' current request, providing him with the spreadsheets my team had prepared. According to Rich's notes from the meeting, Irwin asked many questions but did not offer an opinion on the direction to take.

Rich then noted that it was our opinion that the lease talks should try to be concluded as soon as possible, due to Mr. Wilson's age, and not at a further date down the road, as we had heard had been discussed in Albany. Our main worry was that if Mr. Wilson should die, we would have no way to keep the team in Buffalo after the sale, but also that if Mr. Wilson should outlive the 1998 lease, the weakness of not having hammered out a new deal would be exposed to all.

Rich indicated Irwin agreed with our assessment and was prepared to recommend to the governor that all parties should proceed as rapidly as possible to conclude negotiations. With this recommendation from Irwin, we assumed any future talk of delaying the negotiations until 2013 was put to bed.

Rich and Irwin discussed a few other topics, including the implications of the State and County investing nearly a half-billion dollars in a stadium that was already nearly forty years old. In his notes from the meeting, Rich wrote that they discussed "other options, such as a new stadium," but that a new stadium would be significantly more expensive at this time, and the team did not seem inclined to contribute to the associated costs.

Irwin told Rich it seemed the County had made good progress in fleshing out the needed details of the talks and that he did not intend to reinvent the wheel. Irwin said after speaking with Sam and Steve he intended to talk to our counsel at Nixon Peabody LLP in the next few days to get their perspective on the talks, which we did not object to, and then he would report back to the governor and await his instructions.

Rich informed me that he felt Irwin would be a tremendous help toward getting a new lease signed. He brought a wealth of knowledge on stadium deals and appeared to have the ear of the governor. Finally, Rich answered the question we had pondered earlier—how to pronounce Irwin's last name. "It's pronounced like the bread," Rich confided: "Rye."

Chapter 15

They Want a *What?*

Following the appointment of Irwin Raij by the governor, we assumed lease negotiations would pick up quickly, and it appeared for a time that they might. A meeting was scheduled for September 11 in New York City in which representatives of the NFL would meet with County, State, and team representatives to discuss the status of talks and available financing programs offered by the NFL. We had been asking to meet with the NFL for some time, but with no real State involvement up to that point, it seemed silly to go ahead with it.

Now that the State had "seen the light" and been engaged, it made sense to meet and discuss the matter. While the County's representatives had a good grasp of the G4 financing program, we still felt it made sense to attend the meeting, if for no other reason than to see if the State was truly fully engaged and who would be its lead negotiators.

In order to speed up the process, Rich was working with Irwin and Leecia Eve on setting up a pre-meeting between State and County officials to get everyone on the same page. Rich shipped a copy of the prior lease's closing materials to Irwin for his review, and was working with Liz Burakowski on sending more documents to them when, on August 28, we were advised the State might be backing out of the September 11 meeting with the NFL.

For the next twenty-four hours, no one seemed to know what was happening on the State's end. Irwin was not sure, and emailed Rich letting him know he would check on it. The Bills were getting impatient because they wanted the meeting to be held but did not want to waste their or the NFL's time preparing for a meeting that might not happen. Finally, Leecia emailed after the close of business on August 29 indicating that the State could not attend the meeting on September 11, but they still wanted to meet with NFL representatives and the County before meeting with the NFL.

I was pretty ticked off. It seemed to me the State still didn't know what it was doing. On top of that, getting a meeting with the NFL was not easy considering the 2012 NFL regular season was starting. At this point we were not certain who was in charge of the State's negotiating team—was it Irwin, Leecia, or someone else? We waited to hear from the State.

After a week of silence, Rich and I agreed he would send a "nice" email to Irwin and Leecia, offering to meet at their earliest convenience. Having blocked out September 11 on our calendars for the now canceled NFL meeting, we thought it best to offer to meet them on that date or any other upcoming day that worked for them. So on Friday, September 7, Rich sent Irwin and Leecia an email suggesting those dates to meet. He wrapped up the email by reminding them the football season started "this Sunday at 1 p.m. against the Jets in New Jersey," and suggesting that Irwin should become an avid Bills fan.

There was a reason why Rich noted the season was about to start: we were now entering the final year of the then current lease without any real progress having been made on a new one, and I had previously said publicly I wanted to get a lease done by the start of training camp. I expected to get many media inquiries as to why a new lease had not been agreed to by the start of the season. Thankfully, the game was being played in New Jersey, which meant most local media would be out of town following the team, but I expected an inquiry or two to come soon.

We did not hear much over the weekend, though I saw Lieutenant Governor Robert Duffy at an event, and he told me he was going to play a lead role in the negotiations and would inform Russ Brandon of the development following the game. Prior to becoming the "LG," Duffy was Rochester's mayor and, more important in my book, a lifelong Bills fan. The LG and I had always gotten along very well since the first time I met him in 2010, so I appreciated his upcoming involvement in the talks.

I don't know what the LG said to Russ after the game, or even if they talked, but while we did not get any inquiries over the weekend, they came fast and furious on Wednesday, September 12, after *The Buffalo News'* headline story for the day was "Delay puts Bills lease in jeopardy." Reporter Mark Gaughan pinned the delay solely on the State, noting in the first line that "an inability to get the Cuomo administration to the negotiating table will cause the Buffalo Bills to miss a key deadline to get stadium funding next month from the National Football League. The result is the Bills will not be able to strike a lease deal with New York State and Erie County by the end of the year, as County Executive Mark C. Poloncarz was hoping."

The story had many quotes from Russ on the status of the talks and timing as they pertained to the upcoming owners' meeting. Though Russ never said on the record that the State was to blame for the delay, after reading the article I surmised that if he did not say it off the record, someone at One Bills Drive definitely did. In other media reports from the day that followed, Russ once again noted talks had stalled and had hit a "cone of silence."

I was mad, steaming mad, because the County had been ready, willing, and able to meet at a moment's notice and had made a good faith effort to get a lease done. While *The Buffalo News* story did not lay the blame for the delay at my feet, I knew I would catch a lot of flak for it. I also knew the news story would make the governor go ballistic, something I hoped to avoid, and that he might blame me or my team just as much as the Bills for the story.

I called Russ and noted my extreme disappointment in his statements and for blowing the lid on the State's delays. While not admitting he was the one who told Mark Gaughan that the State was the primary reason for the delay, Russ told me he had heard from the State following his statement, and they had said the same thing. He explained to me that he did it to move things along. While this was probably a smart move on his part, I knew it would infuriate the governor and his team because they were all fearful word would get out that the talks had stalled because of them, and now word was definitely out.

I asked Russ what the Bills were willing to do to repair any damage done with the State. He confirmed what he said in *The Buffalo News* article: the Bills were willing to sign a one-year lease extension under the then current terms to give the State enough time to get its ducks in a row. He noted that it would be impossible to come to terms on the main agreement prior to the next scheduled NFL owners' meeting on October 15, and we needed to show the owners some sort of progress. I was not thrilled with just a one-year extension, but as it appeared the State might never get going I was fine with it, especially if it got the State to agree to something.

My press secretary Peter Anderson's phone was blowing up from media outlets all across North America wanting to know if lease talks were indeed "stalled." We knew we could not hide and say nothing, so we scheduled a press conference for later that morning.

During the nearly hour-long conference, I think I was asked every way possible if *The Buffalo News* story was true, had the negotiations stalled, who was to blame, what had been agreed upon, and even what days we had met. While noting we had not met my self-imposed deadline of getting a deal done before the season began, I stated that we had had productive sessions but were not all in agreement yet. Though I was asked about negotiation details over and over, I would not reveal them or tell the truth as to why a deal had not yet been realized. To show how complicated this transaction was, I brought out Rich's big four-inch-thick bound copy of the prior lease and noted to the press how the upcoming set of agreements would probably be even larger.

At some point I was asked how much longer it would take to get the lease done. I replied that we would get a lease done, and that the Bills had agreed "in principle" to a one-year extension of the current lease if that's what had to happen to get a deal done. My goal was to get a lease agreement done, and we would do just that, even if we needed an extension to do so. I did not say that the extension was all we had agreed on, and most media outlets reported it as just part of the overall story that talks were stalled, but the Associated Press's account of the conference had the one-year extension as the lead.

Soon after the Associated Press story ran across its newswires, I received a call from the Lieutenant Governor and Sam Hoyt, both wondering what the heck was going on. Rich received a call from Leecia Eve, and even Pete Anderson received a call from the governor's press staff. All were adamant that the governor would *not* take the blame for the stalling of the lease, even if they knew the State's failure to be actively involved was the underlying reason.

Each side was steamed over the news coverage, and that turned out to be a good thing because it helped move things along. By the end of September 13, the State agreed to meet with County officials on September 21 in New York City at the governor's offices in Manhattan. In addition, in order to show the State's commitment to the process, either the governor or LG would place a call to Jeff Littmann by the end of the day. We relayed that information to Jeff and waited to hear back from him on the tone and tenor of the call.

Unfortunately, Rich received an email at 9:22 a.m. on September 14 from Jeff Littmann with the subject line, "FYI the call never came." There was no text in the body of the email, just the subject line. That he sent the email with no comment told me Jeff was mad. Rich forwarded that email to Leecia, and I sent a text message to my friend John Maggiore, the chief of staff to the LG, saying someone better call Jeff soon or the talks would not be stalled but dead.

Shortly after noon, Sam Hoyt called Liz Burakowski for Jeff's cell phone number. Sometime thereafter, the LG called Jeff and guaranteed him progress would be made. While this call did not break the ice, it did bring the level of distrust between the parties down a few notches and put everyone back on course to meeting soon.

Over the next few days, Rich, Liz, and I laid out our plan for talking with the State. We agreed it made no sense for Mike Siragusa, Liz, or I to travel to New York City with Rich. Chris Melvin lived in the metro New York area, so he would accompany Rich to the meeting. Rich put together a draft agenda for the meeting, which Liz, Chris, Martha Anderson, Mike, and I all tweaked.

The agenda focused on two main areas: (1) what it would take to get a one-year lease extension agreed to by the parties so it could be presented to the NFL owners for approval at their next scheduled meeting for October 15; and (2) what it would then take to get a long-term lease finalized. We agreed we needed a firm commitment from the State to either agree to sign a one-year extension or begin immediate high-level negotiations to complete a deal before the end of the year.

Somewhere between September 14 and September 20, 2012, Governor Cuomo called me to discuss the situation. For as long as I have practiced law, I have habitually kept contemporaneous notes of major phone conversations or in-person meetings. But for whatever reason, I didn't take notes during this talk, so I don't know the date. I do, however, remember the timing and substance of the call.

While never admitting the State had fumbled the ball for nearly six months, the governor said getting a lease done was of the highest priority to him, and he was assigning the lieutenant governor to the negotiating team, which would also include Leecia Eve and others from his second-floor capital team (the governor's office being located on the second floor of New York State's capital building). The call was cordial, and the governor said he wanted to ensure I understood this was a high priority to him.

I thanked him for his call and for assigning the LG to the negotiating team. I also said that neither of us wanted to be known as the public official in charge when the Bills left town, so it was important that talks move at an expedited pace. He agreed and said he looked forward to a report back on the upcoming meeting scheduled for later in the week. The governor did not go into any detail about the lease, or what his team might offer at the upcoming meeting. I was just glad that he understood a further delay was not acceptable.

I relayed the substance of the call to Rich, who took it as a good sign. No one likes to be on the receiving end of bad press, and *The Buffalo News* story on September 12 was about as bad as it could get for the governor: the reason for a delay was squarely pointed at his office. We both hoped the delays were finally over and the negotiations could start in earnest.

On September 20, as if to highlight the team's desire to get an extension done, Jeff sent to Rich a draft of the "Extension Agreement" that he wished us to forward to the State, as well as a draft agenda for a meeting tentatively scheduled to be held on October 2. Rich informed Jeff he'd pass these items along to the State, though he didn't mention the County and State were meeting the next day.

When I left the office on September 20, I wished Rich good luck and asked him to call me immediately after the meeting. Because of everyone's tight time schedule, instead of meeting at the governor's office's in midtown Manhattan, the parties agreed to meet at a conference room at John F. Kennedy International Airport on Long Island so all could fly in, start the meeting as soon as possible, and then fly out.

The meeting started at noon and finished around 2 p.m. About fifteen minutes later, Rich called me. "Well, you're never going to believe this one," he began. "The State doesn't want to enter into a one-year extension. They are willing to enter into a fifteen-year lease for the Ralph tied to a major renovation, but what they really want is a thirty-year lease tied to the construction of a new stadium in Buffalo."

I'm sure I sounded stunned as this information sunk in. All I could say was, "They want a *what*?"

Chapter 16

Well, Those Were a Crazy Few Days

My phone conversation with Rich did not last long. After my incredulous exclamation, Rich said he wanted to discuss the meeting further with Chris Melvin before he flew back to Buffalo, then put together his notes of the meeting, which he would share with me by the end of the weekend. He did tell me that the LG, Leecia, Irwin, and John Maggiore attended the meeting on behalf of the State, and also that "Howard" joined in for about a half-hour via conference call. I wished Rich safe travels and told him that after hearing this bombshell I looked forward to reading his notes from the meeting and discussing things on Monday.

When he said "Howard," I knew exactly who he meant: Howard Glaser, the director of State Operations and one of the governor's closest advisors. The triumvirate comprising the governor's closest advisors were Joe Percoco, Howard Glaser, and Larry Schwartz. As mentioned earlier, I knew Joe pretty well, but I'd only heard stories about Howard and Larry. What I knew of them was that they were brilliant and totally dedicated to the governor, both having worked for Governor Mario Cuomo, the current governor's father.

Howard had a reputation for being no-nonsense and a very tough negotiator. He was known for getting things the governor wanted accomplished done, which is why he was the Director of State Operations. While the LG might have been the governor's stated point man for the press, I knew if Howard Glaser was involved he was going to be the State's lead negotiator, which suited me just fine as it pertained to dealing with the Bills. I was not certain what it meant with direct dealings between the County and the State.

On Saturday, September 22, Rich called to inform me of some further developments of the night before, as he'd spoken to both Leecia and Irwin late at night. He related that everything appeared to be in play for the State—a new stadium, a further renovation, anything to keep the team in town—and that a conference call was scheduled with Leecia and Irwin the next morning. He said he would update the notes he was compiling with the latest developments and send them to me the next day.

True to his word, as he always was, at 5:11 p.m. on Sunday, September 23, I received an email from Rich with a document containing his typed notes of Friday's meeting and the following developments of that day. Reading through his notes—entitled, "Report: Buffalo Bills–New York State and Erie County–September 21, 2012–New York City, Building 145 at Kennedy Airport"—it was clear to me that the State was not only engaged but would try to dictate the terms to be sought by the governments. Lieutenant Governor Duffy opened the meeting by establishing new ground rules between the State and County. He said the State was starting fresh with a new team and "all past difficulties would be put aside."

When I spoke with Rich about the meeting afterward, he said this wording was the closest the State had come to admitting they had dropped the ball. Rich said the LG was almost apologetic in his opening, and both Chris and Rich felt this was the closest we'd ever get to a "we're sorry for screwing this up" moment.

The LG then stated there would be no more leaks, as if the County had been leaking information. Reading this got me a little hot, as I had spent the better part of the year getting hammered by local media asking for information on the talks without providing any. The closest I came was saying the Bills had agreed in principle to a one-year extension of the lease, which the media already knew from *The Buffalo News* story of September 12. Beyond that fact, the media knew nothing. I wasn't worried about leaks from our end, and didn't like the implication that the County might be the source of information leaked to the press.

The LG went over other "new" ground rules, which were no different from the ground rules we had established with Sam Hoyt and

Steve Gawlik months earlier. Rich's notes also stated that the State was adamant that a joint statement would be issued by the State and County by the end of the day, noting that the two parties had met (though no statement was ever issued).

Then I came to a portion of Rich's report highlighted in yellow that stated, "State also said that it expected that the County will make a significant financial contribution and that the State will pay a smaller percentage of the overall cost then it did under prior lease." Suffice to say, I was a bit steamed at this assumption. This was a three-party agreement, not just two parties, and the County had kept the negotiations alive when the State had crawled along. There was no way we were going to be thrown under the proverbial bus.

Finally, I came to the portion of Rich's notes I was waiting for—what the State wanted as it pertained to a deal. According to Rich's notes and our following discussions, the State would not agree to a one-year extension because they wanted to get a deal done to counter any assertions the State had not been an active participant in the negotiations. Further, the State wanted either a fifteen-year lease at the Ralph tied to a major renovation or a thirty-year lease tied to the construction of a new stadium in Buffalo, and possibly a new convention center and parking ramps. Rich noted the State was "absolutely committed to keeping the team in Erie County."

I asked Rich who had led the State's part of the conversation when these terms were presented—the LG or someone else? He said it varied from the LG and Leecia, but that Howard joined in at this part and seemed to offer more on this topic than the others. If Howard was pushing this, then it meant to both Rich and me that the governor must have given the go-ahead for a potential new stadium.

At this time in the JFK meeting, Rich told me he said the Bills had shown no interest in a new stadium, which was not surprising. Mr. Wilson was at an advanced age, and it made no sense for him to commit to the heavy debt a new stadium would entail. Rich noted that the State and County must have a plan B in the event the Bills would not accept a new stadium option, and that the County and State must be lockstep on this plan B.

Rich also stated that the County was prepared to make a significant contribution, but that the County would not be able to produce the capital necessary for construction of what would likely be a billion-dollar stadium. He noted that the governor's recent passage of a property tax cap for local governments made it almost impossible for the County to pay the debt service needed to finance hundreds of millions in construction costs. As a supporter of the governor's tax cap proposal, I did enjoy the irony that the tax cap might result in the State being forced to assume a greater cost of a renovation of the Ralph or the construction of a new stadium.

Rich also noted that other issues might preclude construction of a new stadium in Buffalo, and we would share those with the State in the coming days. What Rich was hinting at here were the major problems associated with constructing a new stadium in downtown Buffalo: there were not enough open parcels of land to handle a new stadium, and the transportation infrastructure needed to service the stadium without taking a massive amount of then currently occupied land, and spending a tremendous amount of public dollars to do so.

Unbeknownst to the State at the time, in July of 2012, we ordered our Environment and Planning Department's Office of Geographic Information Service (GIS) to prepare an analysis of possible locations for a stadium in Buffalo. We asked the first report to focus on the old Central Terminal location on the east side of Buffalo, as we were getting pressure from some community groups based there to locate a new stadium in that neighborhood.

On August 20, 2012, GIS Director Dale Morris gave Rich and me the first such report, which noted the significant issues involved in building a new stadium adjacent to the location of the old Central Terminal. Dale's report identified the number of parcels and city blocks that would need to be obtained to (1) build a new stadium and (2) handle the footprint of parking lots and ancillary buildings needed for such a stadium. Dale's report noted nearly two hundred acres of land would be needed to replicate the Ralph and its footprint, meaning nearly fifty city blocks would be affected by the construction in the neighborhood.

After we received this report, we asked Dale to have his office perform a similar report for other locations in downtown Buffalo, including those being suggested as sites, such as the outer harbor. We also asked Dale to examine what would happen if we replicated the

Ralph in downtown Buffalo (with no other facilities). Dale informed us before Rich traveled to New York City for the meeting on September 21 that his report would be ready by September 24, 2012. Rich knew this report would be ready soon, but he did not inform the State.

Rich's notes of the September 21st meeting recounted how the State was adamant it would not be able to attend a meeting on October 2, as had been proposed by Jeff Littmann, and the LG would call Jeff immediately after the meeting to offer an alternative date of October 23. The LG did call Jeff and relayed such a message, which was not received well by Jeff. Additionally, the LG noted Jeff said the team was not pleased with the prior week's media stories in which the State seemed to imply that while the State and County were committed to keeping the Bills in Buffalo, the team might not be.

This took everyone by surprise—no one felt such a message had been conveyed. However, everyone knew the team was very touchy about the subject of the Bills staying in Buffalo, and Mr. Wilson had pledged they would stay in town as long as he was alive. So while no one saw this criticism coming, in the end it did not surprise us that the team would take any perceived slight as a critique. If anything, this conversation was helpful: it showed to the State how important it was to keep the Bills happy, at least as it pertained to moving the talks among parties forward. As if to confirm that fact, Leecia called Rich around 10 p.m. on Friday, September 21, to say the governor's office now did not want to delay the October 2 meeting and we should all go under the assumption that we would meet with the Bills that day.

Rich then talked to Irwin from 10:30 to 11:30 p.m. that same night. Irwin advised Rich he was working on cost estimates for a new stadium and he had spoken to officials at Populous to get information about the proposed Minnesota Vikings stadium. The cost was not cheap: approximately $930 million for a retractable roof facility seating about sixty-five thousand, of which ten thousand were club seats. While the $930 million figure included all costs "inside the fence" of the stadium, including a new 1,700 car parking facility, it did not include the cost to acquire land and any necessary transportation improvements, expenses that would surely be large for a downtown Buffalo stadium.

What was interesting about the talk of a new stadium was that neither Irwin nor Leecia expected the Bills to accept such an offer.

Rich noted neither believed the team would accept the proposal, and yet they were moving forth in that direction. This led Rich and I to believe that the idea for a proposing a new stadium in Buffalo came from someone else who worked on the second floor of the state capital building. Either the governor or someone else was pushing the idea of a new stadium.

At 10 o'clock on Sunday morning, September 23, Rich and Chris Melvin held a conference call with Leecia and Irwin on the matters discussed on Friday the 21st. Reading Rich's notes from the meeting, which he emailed to me at 7 p.m. that same day, and discussing the meeting afterward, it was clear the State really was not wedded to any one location for a new stadium or a plan of action. Everyone agreed a forty-acre site would be required to build a new stadium, and that new infrastructure from access roads and parking ramps would be necessary, though no one knew exactly how much at the moment.

The State also discussed the desirability of moving the stadium a thirty-minute drive time closer to the Canadian border crossings. We were not sure what this meant exactly. Did this mean they wanted to move to Niagara Falls or somewhere else in Erie County closer to the Niagara County border crossings? Irwin asked Rich if it was possible to identify a forty-acre site in downtown Buffalo that could accommodate both the stadium and the ancillary services required to service the facility. Rich said we would have a report available from the GIS and we would share it with the group.

The parties agreed to discuss the matter further the next day, including finalizing the ground rules and what the County and State were prepared to offer to the team. A conference call was scheduled for 9:30 p.m. on Monday, September 24.

Early Monday morning, Rich and I discussed in detail the weekend's events and reviewed the report we received from Dale Morris and GIS. The report looked at five possible locations in or near downtown Buffalo: the Central Terminal neighborhood in the east side of Buffalo; the Lower Main Street "Cobblestone" site near Perry and Scott Streets, Michigan Avenue and South Park Avenue; the Outer Harbor of Buffalo; the former Republic Steel site in south Buffalo; and the former Bethlehem Steel site in Lackawanna. Dale's team was able to determine that the rough outline of the stadium bowl and its near perimeter fence was about 17.5 acres. He then superimposed on maps the Ralph as if it had been magically moved to each of the sites.

Every site had its issues. While there was plenty of land to build a stadium and potential parking facilities at the Outer Harbor, Republic Steel, and Bethlehem Steel sites, the transportation infrastructure at each was significantly inadequate to handle the eighty thousand people (patrons and game-day staff) who travel to and from the game. Thus, in addition to building a new stadium in these locations, hundreds of millions and perhaps more than a billion dollars of additional money would be required to build the appropriate transportation infrastructure needed to get people to and from the facility.

Placing the stadium in the Central Terminal/Broadway Market neighborhood on the east side of Buffalo would require the construction of new infrastructure as well, including all new parking facilities, and would essentially require a 150- to 200-acre plot of land to build the facility and related infrastructure. Doing so would require the taking of every parcel of land between Colt Street to the west of Fillmore Avenue and Curtiss Street on the east and from the old terminal on the south to Broadway on the north. In other words, the entire neighborhood, including the Broadway Market, would have to be taken to build the stadium and requisite parking and transportation facilities needed to host a game.

The Cobblestone location was the only location that truly was in downtown Buffalo, and it was the only location downtown large enough to fit a stadium without knocking down large structures. To fit a stadium in this area would require the closing of Perry Street and the placement of the stadium between Scott Street on the north and South Park Avenue to the south. It also truly would not fit in the area between Mississippi and Michigan Avenues, thereby requiring the seizure of office buildings on the corner of Perry Street and Mississippi Avenue (which just happened to be the location of the Empire State Development Corporation's offices in Buffalo) or trying to take land owned by the Seneca Nation of Indians—land tagged for the soon-to-be-constructed Buffalo Creek Casino.

While parking problems would be less of an issue at the Cobblestone Site, as we could tap into the more than 11,500 available parking spaces in the downtown core, the main issue of fitting a stadium there was a problem, though not an insurmountable one, especially if the stadium was reduced in size.

Looking at the report, I realized there was no perfect location for a new stadium. Every potential stadium site identified in the report had significant flaws. Rich and I agreed we needed to get the report in the hands of the State as soon as possible so they understood just what was required to build a new stadium in downtown Buffalo. So Rich summarized the report in an email he sent to Leecia and Irwin that morning, and sent the final report to both later in the afternoon. The reason for the small delay is that we asked Dale Morris and his GIS team to see if they could identify any other forty- to fifty-acre site in downtown Buffalo from the waterfront to the Medical Campus that was available. They could not.

Rich sent the report to Leecia and Irwin at 3:41 that afternoon. Rich, Liz Burakowski, and I then worked on an agenda for the conference call scheduled for 9:30 that night. Once we completed the draft, Rich sent it out to all parties before 6 that evening.

Rich, Liz, and I met at our office at 9 p.m. to discuss how we thought the call would go. I surmised that the State's representatives would have a lot of questions about the GIS report, especially Howard Glaser, assuming he would participate. At 9:30, the conference call began. Leecia immediately informed us she could not participate because something had come up. So for the next hour, we talked with Irwin and Chris Melvin about the GIS report and the issues involved with situating a new stadium in Buffalo. Howard did not participate in the call, nor did anyone else from the State's team, other than Irwin.

And that was the last time we ever heard a word from the State's team about the construction of a new stadium. It was never brought up again. In fact, the next day Rich received a call from Irwin noting the State wanted to present a different proposal on what we (the State and County) should offer the Bills the following week. The new proposal would be solely related to renovation at the Ralph.

Looking back at it now, I believe that when State officials saw the GIS report, they realized the difficulties in constructing a new stadium were too much to overcome. The Bills were not interested in a new stadium—they had told everyone that early in the negotiations. I believed there was no way the team would agree to a new stadium, no matter how good the proposals were, and none of these proposals were all that good. I think State officials realized this and immediately scrapped the idea.

Thus it was important that we had proactively asked our GIS office to prepare the report even before we knew the State was interested in a new stadium. I knew the County was in no position to finance a new stadium, but even if that fact was agreed to by all parties it was still imperative to know the benefits or problems associated with the construction of any new stadium. By having the report at the ready, we were able provide the State with the best available information on the issues associated with proposing a new stadium. While some people called for a new stadium to be built, rather than the Ralph being reno-vated, they generally overlooked the many problems associated with constructing a new stadium in the downtown area. The GIS report succinctly identified those issues.

When Rich and I spoke about the State's latest proposal and how a new stadium was now off the table, I noted how in less than two weeks we went from not much happening, to the story on September 12, to the State wanting to build a new stadium, to finally ending up back to what we had always expected to do: renovate the Ralph. I left the meeting and met with Mike Siragusa and a few others from my staff to review the events of the past two weeks. I said what I think every-one was thinking at the moment: "Well, those were a crazy few days."

Yes, they were, but they were instrumental days on the road to getting a lease agreement done.

Chapter 17

The $400-Million Bomb

From the first meeting with Russ Brandon, Jeff Littmann, and Sam Hoyt, the number one goal for me was ensuring the Bills were the *Buffalo* Bills forever. Knowing the age of Mr. Wilson, I assumed this would be the last lease negotiated under his ownership. It was imperative, therefore, to get an ironclad lease that guaranteed the team would stay in Buffalo following the sale of the team to a new owner.

In fact, during a casual round of golf with Jerry Sullivan and Mark Gaughan of *The Buffalo News* in the summer of 2012, I noted to both, off the record, that my goal was to negotiate a lease with a strong non-relocation agreement and a huge penalty if an attempt to move the team occurred. I remember Jerry saying he found it doubtful the NFL would allow such a lease but that there was no harm in trying.

As we talked with State officials, first Sam and Steve Gawlik, and then Irwin, Leecia, and Howard, we continually stated that any lease we entered into would be deemed a failure unless it prevented the moving of the team upon the sale of it. We knew the State and County's combined expenditure in the 1998 lease was more than $214 million, and passed that information on to the State during the initial talks with Irwin. Any future work might double or even triple the amount spent by the government through the years.

Every State official knew the failure to have a strong non-relocation clause would doom the lease negotiations, and be used against the governor during his reelection campaign in 2014, and invariably mine in 2015. The Bills knew we would seek it, though I don't think they ever entertained what we would eventually request.

Now was the time for the State and County to get on the same page. We needed to proceed with a united front. Any evidence of disunity among us would be noticed by the Bills and invariably result in a weaker lease from the public perspective. So Rich continued his discussions with Irwin and noted we needed to offer a strong response to the Bills to show we were not just united, but that a strong relocation clause was the price the Bills must pay for the State and County's financial commitment.

On Wednesday, September 26, Irwin called Rich and told him that the State agreed to meet with the Bills on October 2 and wanted to present a new proposal. Taking notes, Rich scribbled down on a legal pad what Irwin said: a $220 million total renovation on the Ralph, with the Bills contributing $60 million, the County $69 million, and the State $91 million; the State and County would offer no future operating support; the team would receive naming rights they could monetize if they so chose; and a requirement the team pay a relocation buyout/penalty payable to the State and County equal to the total contribution from both since 1998 and forward.

Upon hearing this proposal, I knew there were issues. First, the Bills expected some sort of operating assistance on an annual basis going forward, and this proposal planned for none. Second, it was doubtful the County could afford such an upfront capital expenditure. The County annually borrowed approximately $30 to 35 million for all of our capital needs: roads, bridges, buildings, and other needs, including the annual contribution for repairing the Ralph. A $69 million County "investment" in renovating the stadium could not be paid for in one year—possibly three, but certainly not in one or two years.

Third, the proposal did not include future contributions for inevitable work that would need to be performed on the facility post-renovation. Even after millions of dollars of work, annual capital maintenance, such as repairing cracks in concrete or even replacing defective toilets, would still be needed. Considering the County owned the facility, there was a justifiable reason for the County to contribute some of the cost for future maintenance.

Finally, any discussion of a buyout penalty would invariably open up the possibility of the team moving, no matter how large the penalty might be. Based on prior NFL leases, relocation fee clauses were acceptable to the league, and having one in our next lease would probably be looked upon with delight from fellow owners who wanted to see the team move. What we needed was a specific performance clause requiring the team to stay in Buffalo, and only if the team could get out of the lease would a substantial penalty be required. It was essential that what we proposed to the team must be a separate non-relocation agreement that included a specific performance clause requiring the team to stay in Buffalo.

It was also important to present the specific performance clause and requisite penalty at the correct time during the negotiations. Proposing such a radical non-relocation agreement at the beginning of the upcoming meeting could cause every other term to be relegated to the back burner. It was essential that what I believed would be a prohibition of moving the team be brought up at exactly the right moment, though I was not sure when that moment would be.

Rich continued conversations with Leecia and Irwin, making sure we were all on the same page and tidying up our combined proposal. We agreed to submit a $220 million renovation plan, with New York paying $91 million, Erie County $69 million, and the Bills the remaining $60 million, with the money to be invested over a three-year renovation period. Under that scenario, the State paid 57 percent of the governmental costs, and the County 43 percent, similar to the 1998 lease agreement. We determined internally we could afford that investment if the County no longer had to pay future operating costs. If operating costs were to be paid, then the County's portion of paying for any renovation would be reduced significantly.

Irwin told Rich that Lieutenant Governor Duffy and Howard Glaser would be attending the meeting. Based on that information, and considering his reputation for being an unblinking negotiator, it was agreed Howard should broach the non-relocation terms, and it was to be done at the end of the meeting. We also agreed on a number to propose as the penalty: $400 million. This figure was derived based on the fact that the figure was arguably close to the combined principal and interest incurred by the State and County for the 1998 lease improvements, the combined operating costs incurred by the State and County on the 1998 lease, and the future cost for improvements. In addition, the figure was sufficiently large to show the seriousness of our commitment to keeping the Bills in Buffalo. Now it was just a matter of sitting down with the Bills, and that meeting was set for the Millennium Hotel in Cheektowaga on October 2, 2012, at 9:30 am.

Heading toward the hotel that day I felt a sense of anticipation that I had not felt before any of the other meetings. I knew the State was fully committed and, short of having the governor present, all of its big guns would be here. There was no backing down now. The presentation we would make today could make or break the negotiations.

Rich and I were joined by Chris Melvin and Mike Siragusa. As we pulled into the hotel's parking lot, I was hoping not to see any media trucks. I knew if media were present, the meeting would be subject to intense scrutiny, and I wasn't sure we would be able to accomplish much with reporters hovering. Thankfully, the meeting had been kept as quiet as a State secret.

Walking into the lobby of the hotel, I saw the familiar sight of the Lieutenant Governor's Chief of Staff, and my longtime friend John Maggiore typing on his Blackberry. Standing outside a meeting room was a plain clothes New York State trooper guarding access to the room. I also saw Paul Lemere, the general manager of the hotel. Paul had graduated from Lackawanna Senior High the year before I did, and while he was not a good friend, I got to know him a bit when we both played on the high school golf team. Paul looked nervous. He said only a few members of his staff actually knew about the meeting and that whatever we needed was at our disposal. I told him the best thing he could do was to keep the meeting as secret as possible.

Walking into the room, I immediately saw Lieutenant Governor Duffy talking on his cell phone. It is tough to miss him, as he is always the tallest person present. In the corner near a table full of doughnuts, bagels, and other breakfast foods were Leecia Eve, Irwin Raij, and Howard Glaser. Rich and I walked up to the three of them and said our hellos. At the opposite side of the room were members of the Bills team, including Jeff Littmann, Russ Brandon, and Eugene Driker, as well as Lou Ciminelli from LP Ciminelli, the project's construction manager, and Scott Radecic and Kelly Kearns from Populous. Scott and Kelly were playing around with a laptop computer and trying to get it hooked up to a projector.

After exchanging hellos and other cordialities, we all sat down and got to business. Jeff Littmann opened and noted how very little infrastructure work had been done of a substantive nature during the past fifteen years to the stadium. Talking it over with Mr. Wilson, he noted they considered pursuing a new stadium, a retrofit or renovation but decided in the end a renovation was the most appropriate way to proceed. Considering this was the first meeting with high-ranking officials present, the Bills wished to go through a PowerPoint presentation of the proposed renovations. With no one objecting to this, Jeff turned over the presentation to Scott Radecic and Kelly Kearns, who proceeded to present basically the same presentation made months earlier when Sam Hoyt and Steve Gawlik represented the State.

I took no notes during Populous's presentation, having seen it before, though I watched the lieutenant governor, Irwin, Leecia, and Howard all scribbling furiously on their legal pads. The State's team asked a few questions, similar to the questions we'd asked months before. Following Populous's presentation, Jeff started saying things we knew would cause trouble when we would present our proposal to take all future operating support off the table. Jeff stated that there "aren't any new revenue areas" and that they "need to protect the current revenue" arrangement. Jeff noted without any new additional subsidy, the team would need to come up with an additional $5 million in incremental revenue somewhere, and increase ticket prices to bring in an additional $2 million to meet the expectations of the league.

Jeff then spoke of structural issues related to the stadium and how the team foresaw future renovations taking place. Lou Ciminelli discussed a few structural issues as well, and said his company was planning for all renovations to be completed over three seasons, with the vast majority of work to be completed in years two and three. At this point Lou, Scott, and Kelly left the meeting; it was now time to begin serious negotiations.

Based on what Rich and Irwin had previously discussed, it was agreed I would open the discussion from the view of the public sector. I noted how after a number of fits and starts we were now in a position to get a lease negotiated in a short period. Everyone from the

State and County was committed to resolving the discussions soon, and were united in the direction to take. I discussed the current financial status of the County and how the County would be in no position to offer operating support if a large capital contribution was expected. I also noted that any lease had to include a strong, enforceable non-relocation provision; otherwise it would be unacceptable from not only the officials' eyes, but for the greater public as well.

Lieutenant Governor Duffy then offered the State's vision of what it expected in a lease, which pretty much followed what I said: to protect the public's investment in the facility, the team must agree to a non-relocation agreement that left no question as to where the home of the team would be—in Orchard Park, New York. The LG also wanted the Bills to know there would be no question as to whether the State was engaged through not only his participation but by noting all discussions from today would be relayed back to the governor. For good measure, the LG noted he had been a Bills fan since he was a child, and he would consider getting a long-term lease done one of the crowning achievements in his public career.

Jeff followed, noting the team's endgame took into account the governments' issues. He said, "Ralph Wilson's legacy is tied to the Buffalo Bills being in Buffalo." The team just wanted a "fair opportunity to earn themselves into the third quartile of NFL revenue," he said. While they will "protect the taxpayer's investment," according to Jeff, we "need to get 2013 put away soon or the NFL will step in to resolve the issue." I took this to be Jeff's way of saying if we do not get a one-year extension done soon, the NFL might force the team to take actions it would prefer not to take, though I was not exactly sure what those might be.

At this point, Howard started to make our formal proposal. He stated when you take into account interest, the old deal cost the State and County $218 million (which was more than we'd previously determined; I'm not sure how he came up with that figure), and this new deal could cost the governments more than $482 million in the long term (a figure we in the County did not dispute in the meeting but which I believed was inflated). He then went line by line through our proposal: a $220 million renovation with the governments paying $160 million and the Bills $60 million; the construction period being three years based on a fifteen-year lease; stadium-naming rights to be determined; an "abandonment fee"; and then he surprised the Bills when he said there would be no further operating expenses or working capital paid for by either the State or County.

Howard explained why the State believed the operating subsidy should end. I then spoke on behalf of the County. I noted how things had changed in Erie County since the 1998 lease: the County's property tax rate had decreased significantly since 1998; the 2005 Red/Green Fiscal Crisis had destroyed the County's finances then and were just getting back to normal; and we were now under the watchful eye of a control board. Mostly, however, we simply could not afford an operating subsidy under the current fiscal situation based on what the County was willing to contribute in construction expenses.

Looking at the Bills' negotiating team, it was quite evident they were not expecting us to take future operating expenses off the table. In fact, Jeff Littmann looked visibly perturbed. He said the reason the working capital subsidy was put in was "to offset the lack of revenue to be generated in the Buffalo media market compared to other NFL markets." He said operating subsidies were created "because of the low ticket prices charged and the inability to raise prices." He then said something I'm not sure he intended to say but that let the proverbial cat out of the bag: the team ranked "29th in revenue and there was no way to make it up."

Howard made a very persuasive argument as to why you do not see public investments as operating subsidies in other businesses. While a government might subsidize the construction of a facility, it does not provide direct assistance solely to be used for salaries and other operating expenses. The public expects its money to go to other areas.

Exasperated, Jeff Littmann said, "I can't make that work."

We had been meeting for almost two hours at that point, so Rich recommended we take a break and caucus among our respective teams. We on the County and State's team agreed to leave the room to the Bills, and we'd would find another place to talk.

I went out and talked to John Maggiore, who sat quietly in the background during the meeting, observing everything. John is one of the smartest people I know and has been involved in many important government matters over the years, so I looked forward to hearing his impression of the meeting to that point.

He told me the team certainly looked shocked when we took the operating subsidies off the table. He noted they were not in a position to respond to the request because they never expected it. Rich joined us and said in all of his years of dealing with Jeff he never saw him as taken aback as he was at the end. We all agreed this was a risky tactic to take, but it certainly put us in the driver's seat, as the team could not contemplate a new lease without future operating expenses. This could be used as a bargaining chip for other areas.

After about a half-hour break, spent on our side with all participants caucusing and typing on smart phones, we reconvened. Considering the Bills had had the last, exasperated word, Jeff started again. The team "cannot support this structure," he said. He would not even "present it to the owner," and he doubted "the league would even support it." He then said something I believe he was using as a threat to us that the team could eventually move, by noting "existing ownership does not support us." Jeff was not referring to Mr. Wilson supporting his negotiating team but to the rest of the NFL owners supporting the Bills organization.

Jeff then went into the minutia regarding the operating revenues of the team, and how the organization needed $10 to $11 million per year to meet its current standard. He then said something that was very telling: it really did not matter how much the governments paid toward the renovation, because the operating subsidy was more important for the team. As Jeff went through his calculations, Lieutenant Governor Duffy asked whether the team would open its books to us so we could confirm the team's need for an operating subsidy. Jeff responded that even if the team wanted to do so, "the league [would] not allow our books to be opened."

Positively, Jeff did say if we could figure out the subsidy portion of the equation, the team was amenable to the renovation split being $160 million for the governments and $60 million for the Bills. The LG and Howard both responded they were unable to approve anything until we resolved the subsidy issue.

No one from the County said anything at this point. There was no need, and we did not want to pile on at this point. I glanced over at Russ, who looked stunned. Neither he nor anyone else from the Bills expected this hardline approach. It was time to take another break so that hotel workers could exchange the stale doughnuts for sandwiches and cookies.

Sitting in the lobby, the State's and County's teams agreed we had totally shocked them. They had not contemplated the loss of the operating expenses, and we were not sure they knew how to respond. We decided our group needed to offer something to the Bills to show we would negotiate in good faith and see if we could agree on something other than the renovation split so as not to destroy the discussions. It was decided the LG would ask if there were any new benefits the State could help them with going forward. Then Rich and Howard would inquire as to whether the team was amendable to reducing the renovations in exchange for offering operating support.

Before settling back in our seats, I walked over to the snacks table, now covered with a spread of lunchmeats, cheeses, breads, and cookies. I started making a sandwich when Russ approached to do the same. I asked him what he thought, and he joked that he "preferred Sam and Steve not negotiating to this." I told him there was no way the County could afford to pay an operating expense subsidy if we had to pay $50 to $60 million in capital costs. I think he got the message because he said simply, "I know."

Back at the table, the LG spoke first, asking the team if there was any way New York State could assist the team in areas we had not addressed. Russ noted the team for years had tried to partner with the New York Lottery to generate additional revenue for both: the lottery would sell scratch off or other tickets with the Bills logo on it, and both would share the proceeds from the sales. He also mentioned that the team was dealing with counterfeit vendors of goods and that the State could take a more active role in stopping it. He asked for help enforcing ticket-scalping laws and some other minor things. The LG said the State was certainly amenable to helping out with all those issues, and immediately tasked John Maggiore to reach out to each appropriate State agency to address them.

At this point, Rich and Howard tag-teamed Jeff regarding the amount of renovations to be performed and what we needed to do to make a deal happen. Jeff mentioned the team could revisit the amount of renovations, but that, for now, they were more interested in discussing a one-year extension of the current lease. That would give them the time needed to look at all aspects of the renovations.

Howard talked about the renovations and how the State and County were amendable to reducing the amount of our investment on the renovations and redirecting that funding to other needs, but he never mentioned the extension. I then said, "I think we have accomplished much. We both understand the other side's desires much more clearly, but for the County and State, the economics of it all must work." Jeff said he had a much better understanding of the State and County's position and that he would go back and look at what could be done to meet our needs. As such, the meeting ended on an amicable note.

I walked over to talk to Russ. Of everyone involved, I talked the most with Russ. This made sense: Russ and I were in similar positions—the chief executive officers of our respective organizations—and were the same age, so we had things in common. While talking to Russ, I looked over at Howard, who was talking with Jeff. Howard was telling him something, and then I saw Jeff's mouth open as if he wanted to say something but couldn't. He looked stunned. Russ noticed it too and said he would get back in touch with me soon. The team's representatives then left the room.

The State and County's teams stayed in the conference room and caucused for a bit as we put on our coats. I told Howard it looked like he had dropped the $400-million bomb on Jeff. He had—and Jeff was shocked and angry. Howard said Jeff responded that if the State and County were going to bring up such an important term, it should have been part of the main discussion, not as an afterthought. We agreed that regardless of what Jeff thought, we had probably handled it well in that the team was now flustered. We also agreed that as a negotiating team we had worked very well together during the meeting. Everyone spoke at the appropriate moment, and we never showed any disagreement. While we might not have had achieved an agreement, we had accomplished much in that we now had the team thinking on our terms and not theirs.

As we left, we expected the Bills to offer a counter to our proposals, and we planned to push for a meeting soon. Driving away, I kept seeing the look on Jeff's face and could hear the Gap Band in my head singing, "You dropped a bomb on me, baby"—a $400-million bomb.

Now, the big question remained: would our bomb lead to the non-relocation clause we wanted, or had the negotiations been blown up beyond the point of no return?

Chapter 18

Detroit

After the October 2 meeting I expected some days to pass without discussions between the parties. In fact, other than some internal discussions by County officials, all was quiet on the discussions front. Or so I thought.

On Thursday, October 11, 2012, Jeff Littmann emailed Rich Tobe at 9:35 a.m. to request a call to "catch up." Rich was not available in the morning and did not immediately call Jeff. In the meantime, Howard received an email from Jeff at 10:51 a.m. that was much more ominous than the one he sent to Rich. Jeff's email stated:

> The NFL Owners Fall Adjourned Meeting takes place Tuesday, October 16th, in Chicago. In advance of that meeting the Stadium Committee will be briefed by NFL staff in detail on the state of our negotiations. The rest of the Owners will be given a very brief update by NFL staff which will state that "little progress has been made" and that the focus has moved to a "one-year extension."
>
> Following the meeting, as mentioned in my email to you on October 8, we will be ceasing the design development work. Our lead architect, Populous, is aware of this but has not yet communicated it to the various subcontractors.
>
> We will not be able to control the narrative with this many outside parties aware that our talks have not pro-

gressed. Scott Berchtold is our Sr. V.P. of Communications. I would suggest that your P.R. staff work with Scott to see if we can agree on an appropriate way to communicate to our stakeholders as these events unfold.

Howard forwarded Jeff's email to Rich and others at 3:55 that afternoon. It was our first indication that Howard and Jeff had been communicating in some form, at least by email, since the meeting on October 2.

Then, at 5:28 p.m., Jeff sent Rich the following e-mail: "Rich—The Stadium and Finance Committees report at 9:20 p.m. Chicago time on Tuesday. Jeff." Without saying much, Jeff was letting us know that the NFL owners would be meeting on Tuesday, October 16, and would be expecting a positive report from the team.

What I found interesting was the difference in tone of the two emails. Jeff's email to Howard sounded somewhat threatening, while his email to Rich was more matter of fact. It indicated to me that Jeff not only trusted Rich but may have been trying to use him to spur the State into quick action.

After I discussed the matter with Rich, he called Jeff and spent the next hour talking with him. It was at this point Rich learned that Howard and Jeff had just talked and Jeff suggested having everyone meet in Detroit the next day to try to resolve the major sticking points. Rich finished his call and then called me. I remember hearing Rich saying the other parties wanted to meet the next day at Ralph Wilson's business offices in Detroit, and he thought it was important to take them up on their offer. He asked for my permission to go, and suggested Mike Siragusa and I go as well.

Unfortunately, I could not attend this meeting, and neither could Mike. I was scheduled to release my 2013 County Budget on Monday, October 15, and would be meeting with *The Buffalo News'* editorial board on Friday the 13th to discuss the budget's projections and our plans for the future. After a few quick calls, we agreed Rich would go to Detroit and be joined by Chris Melvin, and by Joseph McMahon from my office. Joe is my key constituent relations officer, attends many functions with me, and is generally aware of what is going on in most County departments. Joe had not been part of prior meetings, but I'd kept him apprised of the status of the discussions. When Joe got the call telling him he'd be driving with Rich tomorrow, it took no more than a millisecond for him to say "Yes!"

Rich and I discussed a few parameters on the negotiations, including agreeing to continue the operating subsidy if the total construction costs were reduced. I also suggested inclusion of a rental clause and an annual rental payment to be made by the Bills (they did not pay rent under the 1998 lease). I thought it was only fair that if the team subleased the facilities, it should pay rent in a to-be determined amount—otherwise it was not a lease but a gift of the use of the facility. Rich agreed, and we made this a component of future discussions.

So, early on Friday, October 13, Joe and Rich drove the four-plus hours to Detroit, while I met with *The Buffalo News* editorial board. My meeting with the board was just ending as the meeting in Detroit was beginning. Rich called me just before 1 p.m. to say Howard, Irwin, and the LG were there on behalf of the State (they flew in on the State's plane), while the Bills were represented by Jeff and Eugene Driker.

For the next couple of hours, I waited patiently for a report from Rich. I texted Joe for any update, and he replied that he'd spent portions of the day outside the room returning calls from others and obtaining information Rich and Chris Melvin requested. According to my notes, at 3:58 p.m., Rich called me to say they were making very good progress and the Bills appeared to be caving on the total amount of renovations to be performed, but would not forgo receiving the operating, game-day, and working capital subsidies. He noted the State and County were not giving up the fight for no future operating support, at least for the moment. He also said the Bills wanted a seven-year agreement because of the reduced renovation.

Hearing that, I told Rich it was too short a period. A seven-year lease would be widely panned if the team could leave with no further obligation to the community. He also told me the Bills were becoming more amenable to including the $400-million penalty clause in the final agreement because they now understood the goal of the State and County was to have a specific performance requirement, and the $400 million would be paid only if the team was allowed to move by a court of law. This clause was to protect the community in the event Mr. Wilson died and a new owner then attempted to move the team.

Mr. Wilson had no intention to move the team. With an understanding that the County and State were not trying to penalize the team, but instead protect it from being moved upon Mr. Wilson's death, the negotiations were progressing. He told me all parties were eager to work out the details so they might be in Detroit the rest of the day.

For the next two hours, I waited again for Rich's call, texting and calling Joe for occasional updates. Joe mentioned he was surprised at how modest Mr. Wilson's headquarters were—not much different from offices you might find in a suburban office park. The only way you knew this office was for an NFL team were the AFC championship trophies on display in the waiting area.

Around 6:00 p.m., Rich called to tell me there was a chance they could have an agreement in principle by the end of the day. The Bills were now amenable to a seven- or ten-year agreement, and the State had compromised by agreeing to pay future operating expenses through the working capital account, though both the County and State were seeking a reduction in the annual operating expense payments. He said the parties had now agreed to reduce the capital renovations of the Ralph to $130 million, with the Bills paying somewhere around $30 million.

According to Rich, a few more details needed to be resolved, but it seemed like they were close—if not to an actual agreement, at least close enough for the Bills to be able to report to the NFL the following week that negotiations were progressing well and an agreement was imminent. He said they planned on meeting for another session and would call me back when they were done for the day.

That night I had planned to go to dinner at Hutch's in Buffalo with Christa Vidaver, my girlfriend at the time. About 7:30 p.m., as our entrees were being served, Rich called and said there appeared to be an agreement in principle among the parties. I immediately looked at Christa, whom I had told about the meeting in Detroit, and whispered across the table that we might have an agreement. Being a big Bills fan, a huge smile appeared on her face. I then stepped away from the table to talk to Rich.

He noted everyone was pretty burned out after a long day but that major obstacles had been overcome and the parties had agreed on almost all the major terms: length of the lease (ten years, with a one-time buyout option for the team in the seventh year, though the

Bills still far preferred a seven-year lease); the amount of renovations ($130 million); and issues related to the annual operating subsidies. One issue not agreed on yet was a requirement the team stay during the term of the lease prior to or after any seventh-year option, and if they tried to move and in fact did move, the team would pay a penalty of $400 million. Rich said that a few issues remained open and that everyone had agreed to revisit those in a day or two, with Jeff to send everyone a recitation of the agreed-upon terms the next day.

Rich said he was very tired and needed to review his notes, as he'd probably missed something to tell me, and that we would talk tomorrow. Joe told me later that as soon as they hit the road, Rich fell asleep and slept most of the trip back to Buffalo.

On Saturday, October 13, at 1:39 p.m., Jeff sent Rich, Howard, and the LG an outline of the terms agreed on by the parties the day before. Rich forwarded the message to me a few minutes later. It was apparent that while much had been accomplished, there was still work to be done.

First, as Rich had stated, there was no mention of a separate non-relocation agreement in the document. In fact, Jeff's email stated, "the new term will be either (i) a seven years base with an option on the part of the team to extend the term an additional three years, or (ii) a 10-year term with an option on the part of the team to terminate the last three years. The seven-year base period will be non-terminable, will not be subject to a buyout right, will be subject to a specific performance right on the part of ECSC (Erie County Stadium Corporation, the party which actually subleases the stadium to the team) and will be further subject to a liquidated damages clause for breach." While the team had agreed in principle to the specific performance clause, they had not yet agreed to the $400 million liquidated damages clause, though some figure would be paid, and they had not agreed to a stand-alone non-relocation agreement.

I knew we needed a separate non-relocation agreement. Under federal bankruptcy law, a lease can be terminated during any bankruptcy procedure. If a future owner filed for bankruptcy, and all non-relocation provisions were contained solely in a lease, the lease could be voided, thus terminating the non-relocation provisions as well. It was imperative the Bills agree to a separate document that prohibited relocation of the team, which should also contain the specific performance clauses and the penalty in the event the team was allowed by a court of law to move. This document would be the community's greatest protection to the team leaving. This was non-negotiable on our part.

Further in the message, Jeff noted that if the agreement was to be ten years, and not just seven, then the Bills could buy out the remaining three years for a payment of $28,363,500. At first glance, this seemed a strange amount to be agreed on, but it represented the approximate amount remaining of the amortized payments related to the State's and County's investments in stadium renovations. In other words, if the team elected to leave, they would pay the State and County back the amount the State and County would pay in principal and interest still remaining on the bonds sold to pay for the renovations. I was not thrilled with the provision, but if it was the linchpin the team needed to close a deal, I could live with it. In the then current (1998) lease, the Bills could have left for less than the salary of a backup linebacker in any of the prior few years. So if this is what it took to get a deal done, I could accept it.

The team agreed to $130 million in stadium renovations, scrapping the plans to redesign the west end-zone and expansion of the north and south fifty-yard line areas. The parties agreed to split the $130 million cost of the renovations as follows: $95,545,000 for the State and County, and $35,455,000 for the team. The parties also agreed to various figures for future years operating, game-day, and working capital expense accounts. This was a major compromise by the State, which truly preferred not to continue paying these amounts. The team also agreed to pay $800 thousand (adjusted in future years for inflation) for rent and annual maintenance of the facility. While the County was primarily responsible for past maintenance, the Bills did pay for some, though they were not required to do so. Now we had a requirement that the team pay for some of the future costs of the stadium's upkeep.

Reading through the term sheet, I wished I could have attended the meeting to negotiate the terms in person. Then I chuckled to myself, as it occurred to me that if I had been present perhaps no agreement would have been reached. Regardless, I was pleased to see tremendous advancement in the talks, and felt like an agreement in principle could be announced very soon.

However, one final attachment to Jeff's email spelled trouble—he still wanted the State and County to sign a one-year extension of the then current lease, which would be voided if we signed the final agreements. This was unacceptable to the State, and now that we had reached mutual agreement on many important terms, it seemed to me unnecessary as well. The one-year extension would only be necessary if we were unable to resolve the major terms, and now they seemed resolved. This would be a further sticking point.

On Sunday, I sat down with Rich to talk over the meeting. While a tremendous amount of progress had been made, significant issues remained to be resolved. One that Rich had not mentioned to me while in Detroit was that the State was asking the County to put in a greater share of total costs in the project than the County had before. In fact, the State was seeking a fifty-fifty split between the State and County for all capital infrastructure and operating expenses associated with the lease. In the 1998 lease, the County paid no capital component and about 40 percent of the operating expense.

We had expected the County to contribute something toward the capital renovations of the stadium, but not 50 percent of the government's portion of renovations. In fact, using the 1998 lease as a baseline, we expected a similar 57 to 43 percent split between the State and County, with the State responsible for the larger share. A fifty-fifty split for the cost of renovations and future operating subsidies would not only be unfair in my eyes, but would be unaffordable for the County for many reasons, including the tax cap recently passed by Governor Cuomo.

Rich told me his conversations with Howard Glaser on this subject went nowhere, so it would be up to me to discuss this with the governor and lieutenant governor. However, considering we had a phone conference scheduled with the State's team on the afternoon of Tuesday, October 16, Rich suggested I wait before reaching out to see if the State might change its position during our phone conference.

On Tuesday morning, prior to our call with the State, the County's team gathered for a conference call with our counsel from Nixon Peabody. Rich started the call by informing everyone about the meeting in Detroit, and how a number of issues were still outstanding, including the percentages to be contributed between the State and County, and that Howard had sent him an email stating he wanted to close the transaction within "three to four days." Once he said that, I could hear an audible "gasp" on the end of the phone from one of the Nixon Peabody lawyers (there were four on the call). The gasp told everyone what that lawyer thought of the proposition—that it would be impossible to complete the transaction in such a short time.

Chris Melvin noted that all kinds of issues still remained on the table, and even if we were able to resolve them by the end of the day, which was impossible because the Bills were unavailable, the earliest a set of draft documents could be prepared would be in a week. Everyone understood that this was the usual way members of the Cuomo Administration negotiated deals in Albany: resolve the major terms and get the deal announced ASAP, even if a term or two remained in question.

But we were not talking about last-minute budget dealings between the governor's office, the Assembly, and the Senate (known in Albany parlance as "The Big Ugly"). This was a complicated deal with a private entity that would require approval from the National Football League. We could not screw up the terms; if we did, it could result in losing the team one day. Everyone on the call agreed it was imperative to get the State to slow down from any effort to try to finalize the deal until all major terms were agreed on by the Bills, and the split of contribution had been settled between the State and County. Rather than make a full-on assault on the call, we would discuss it, and then leave it to me to negotiate with the governor, or if need be, the lieutenant governor, over the issues.

At 4 o'clock that afternoon, Mike Siragusa and I joined Rich in his office as he dialed into the call. Based on my notes, between State representatives and our respective counsel, eleven people were on the call. Howard, who led the discussion, said the most disconcerting item to him was that the Bills still wanted to sign a one-year extension, which the State refused to accept. Howard felt if this issue were resolved we could have the deal completed in "three or four days."

Chris Melvin then brought Howard and other members of the State's team back to earth. No one had more experience negotiating with the NFL than Chris on either the State or County's team, and everyone on the call knew it. He noted it was doubtful the team and the NFL would agree to such an expedited timeline. Chris pointed out that we must have a separate non-relocation agreement, and the team had still not accepted that arrangement, and even if it did, it would require NFL approval before we could announce it.

Additionally, Chris noted a definitive construction agreement would have to be negotiated among all parties, which would include the funding percentages and the times to disburse money to pay for the renovations. Chris noted documents could be turned around by his firm in a week once the terms were finalized by all. He suggested his firm take the lead in redrafting the two main leases of the stadium (lease of the County to the State and then the sublease of the State to the Bills), as well as a non-relocation agreement, providing the drafts to our working group for everyone's review, and, once we were all satisfied, transmitting those draft documents to the Bills for their review.

Irwin Raij was on the call and said that "sounds like a workable plan." When Irwin said it was a "workable plan," this must have given Howard the cover he needed to back off from his prior demand because Howard then stated he agreed to the plan as well. Rich and I both smiled, knowing we had pulled Howard back from his "let's get this done in three days" without his having to admit to the group it was unworkable to do so. It also gave me some time to try to negotiate the split in costs between the State and the County.

As I've said before, if you wanted to speak to the governor, you needed to talk to Joe Percoco, because Joe was the governor's gatekeeper. So, on the morning of October 17, I called Joe Percoco at the governor's office in New York City in attempt to speak to Governor Cuomo. Joe was not in the New York office, so I was switched to the Albany office. After waiting a few moments as they searched for Joe, I was told he was unavailable and asked if I would like to leave a message. I said I wished to speak to the governor in regards to the split of the State and the County's share of the Ralph Wilson Stadium renovations.

Then I waited for Joe's return call . . . and waited, and waited. On October 21, I spoke to my chief of staff Jennifer Hibit to see if she had spoken to Joe on any topic during the past few days, as they occasionally talked about government and other topics. She said she had not.

So on the morning of Monday, October 22, I called Lieutenant Governor Duffy on his personal cell phone and left him a message similar to the one I had left with Joe a few days earlier. I then sent a text to John Maggiore, the chief of staff to the LG to let him know I had left a message with his boss, and John responded "Got it." Finally, I called Joe Percoco again, this time on his personal cell phone and left a similar message, except this time I told him I had reached out to the LG as well. I then exchanged a few texts with John Maggiore again, who told me the LG was not able to speak now but I should be hearing from someone soon.

A few hours later, around 7:30 p.m. and while attending a function at Curly's in Lackawanna, I received a call on my cell phone from the 518 area code, which is the area code for Albany. It was Joe Percoco. Unfortunately, my phone immediately died as we started talking. I then asked to borrow my chief of staff's phone, as she had joined me at the function. I called Joe from Jennifer's phone, reached him at his Albany office, and we proceeded to discuss the terms of the deal.

Joe was under the impression the "deal was done" and with it being "done," he did not want the County to "screw it up." I stated while a framework was in place, we needed to resolve a number of issues between the State and County and the Bills, as well as the split between the State and County. I told him of the open terms with the team, which seemed to surprise him a bit, and reminded him that with the tax cap now in place, and the County still operating under the oversight of a fiscal control board, it would be impossible for me to agree to a greater share of the costs for the County because (1) I could not afford it without cutting other services, and (2) I did not want to say the County would be forced to go over the governor's tax cap because we were forced to accept a deal that raised taxes.

Upon hearing that, Joe said the governor thought the deal was a good one, but he understood our issues. He said Howard would call me tomorrow to discuss the split of expenses in greater detail, or he would put Howard on the phone right then. I told him I was standing outside a restaurant in Lackawanna and I would prefer discussing it with Howard in the morning when I was sitting at my desk and I could review the spreadsheets and analysis in detail. He agreed it made more sense to do it that way, told me Howard would call me after 9 a.m., and with that we ended the call.

I handed Jennifer her phone back and told her I had better get a good night's sleep because I would be spending a good portion of the morning negotiating with Howard. Before heading to bed, however,

I sent an email to Rich Tobe and Budget Director Robert Keating, detailing our discussions and asking Bob for his analysis on the latest split discussions with the State as it pertained to the 2013 budget and our four-year financial plan.

Knowing that Howard was usually punctual, I arrived at the office the next morning around 8:30, reviewed my notes and various spreadsheets on proposed contributions, and waited for Howard's call. I also read *The Buffalo News*, which had a headline story about a proposed new billion-dollar-plus development and stadium to be built on the City of Buffalo's outer harbor by a private consortium, with the assistance of hundreds of millions of dollars of government assistance. I had just about finished the story when, at 9:15, my receptionist called me and said Howard Glaser was on the line.

Howard started by making a joke about a story out of New York City that day, and I asked him if he'd seen the stadium story in *The Buffalo News*. Howard said he had not, so I related to him the details and sent him a link to the story. We both knew a new stadium was a nonstarter for the Bills and, with a deal close, we agreed to focus on a new lease if media should ask for a response to the story.

About that time, at 9:25, I received an email from Bob Keating with his projections on the impact of the proposed fifty-fifty split on the budget and four-year financial plan compared to our original 57 to 43 percent expectation. Quickly scanning his message, I could see what I had hoped to see: under the latest proposal we would pay *less* for the operating and game-day expenses than we had under the past lease, even in a scenario where we paid a fifty-fifty split of operating expenses between the State and County (though with the County now contributing $30 million plus in capital improvements, we would pay more per year in the long run). With this in mind, and the pleasantries between Howard and me over, we spent the better part of the hour going over the County's budget, the tax cap, the expectations of the County and the State, and various financial scenarios.

Howard said the State felt it was fair for the parties to pay for everything in a fifty-fifty split. I then reminded him of a conversation he had previously with Rich Tobe where he agreed to a renovation capital split of 57 percent for the State and 43 percent for the County. Because of this previous assurance from Howard, we'd assumed all public contributions would be split the same way: current renovations, future capital expenses, and operating expenses.

Howard did acknowledge the previous conversation with Rich, but he noted that was made under the assumption the renovations would be much larger, and therefore more expensive. I reminded him that because of the tax cap, I could not pay for the County's share of the renovations out of the current operating budget—I would have to borrow funds through a bond to pay for it. I noted how a fifty-fifty split would not work with the budget I had just released, as everything was predicated on the County paying 43 percent. The only way I could afford a fifty-fifty split for future operating costs was if the County's portion of the renovation expenses was significantly reduced, because it would then lessen the principal and interest related to our debt service to pay for it in future years.

I knew fighting with Howard, and by association Joe Percoco and the governor, would not endear me with the governor's team, but I had no choice. I knew what we could afford, and we could not afford a fifty-fifty split for all costs associated with a new lease, especially with the governor's new tax cap in place. While our future operating and game-day expenses would in fact be less than what the County paid for in the 1998 lease, our total expenditure would be substantially higher because of the costs associated with the County's portion of the renovation. So I had no choice but to fight it out.

I must have said something right because Howard eventually said he would look at the schedules we previously provided to him once again and get back to me in a few days. I hung up the phone feeling confident the State would go back to paying more of the total cost, though I was not yet sure it would accept the 57 to 43 percent split.

Not long after hanging up the phone with Howard, I received a call from Lieutenant Governor Bob Duffy. He apologized for taking a few days to return my calls and said he was checking to see if Howard called and how it went. I told him it was a good call and that I thought he now understood the County's financial predicament.

I assumed the governor's office had planned for the LG to call me as the "good cop" after I had talked to Howard's "bad cop." Regardless, I always enjoyed taking to the LG—he's not only a Bills fan through and through, but a good man. I think I disarmed him when I said the call with Howard went well, so instead of talking about the percentage split we discussed other items relating to the lease discussions. Importantly, he said that if we could wrap up the few outstanding, though important, terms, we could be holding a press conference to announce the new lease "after Election Day, around Veterans Day." This directly contradicted Howard's earlier "three to four days" expectation, and told me the Cuomo administration knew we were at least two or three weeks or more out from announcing the transaction.

Additionally, Bob relayed to me his thoughts on the Detroit meeting and how, in his view, "Jeff moved more than we thought" he would. We both agreed the team came down significantly from their original requests, and it appeared they were just as desirous of getting a deal done as we were. This indicated to us that perhaps Mr. Wilson's health was worse than we had originally thought, and the team wanted to get a deal done before he passed.

At the end of the conversation, he told me to call him if I did not get a response from Howard in the near future, but he expected a quick one as Howard wanted to wrap up the deal. I thanked him for the call and for his great work in getting a deal done. I told him I looked forward to standing with him when we announced the new deal in a few weeks.

At the same time, unbeknownst to either of us, somewhere in the Caribbean Sea, Tropical Storm Sandy was gaining strength.

Chapter 19

Sandy and Troubles at Home

On October 25, 2012, my team received an email notice from our counsel Martha Anderson that Irwin Raij and the State's counsel had reviewed the documents Nixon Peabody had prepared and wanted to make further revisions to them. At approximately the same time as our email exchange, Hurricane Sandy, now a category 3 hurricane, was making landfall on Cuba. None of us thought anything about the hurricane at this point. Hurricanes hit the Caribbean and southeastern United States every year, but rarely do they affect New York.

Later that day, Chris Melvin informed everyone via email the Bills had now imposed a date of getting a one-year extension signed by November 15, 2012. Because we were so close to a deal, we assumed we would have the basic terms all settled and thus could ignore the date completely. At the rate we were going, we might be done by November 1, 2012, so why would we work on a one-year extension if the main terms were complete?

About the same time I read Chris's email, I also saw the first reports that Hurricane Sandy was projected to strike the eastern seaboard. I still did not think much of it. On October 26, however, as the warnings became much more significant about Hurricane Sandy's potential, I contacted our emergency services commissioner for more information on the storm's potential. Over the next three days, Erie County, like most other communities, took action to prepare for the hurricane's onslaught and inform the public to take protective measures.

Howard Glaser moved from being the lead negotiator for the State on the Bills lease into his primary role as director of state operations in leading the state government's efforts to prepare for the storm.

On the morning of October 29, when it became apparent the storm would strike the metro New York City region, I sent Howard Glaser and Joe Percoco a short email: "Great job on the storm prep—Good luck today." Three minutes later, Howard sent a text saying thank you. At this time, I doubt he realized the full extent of damage the storm would wreak later that evening. I know I didn't.

Hurricane Sandy was one of the worst natural disasters to strike the United States and the Caribbean. It caused tens of billions of dollars of damage and resulted in more than 200 deaths, 157 of them in the United States. Completing a lease was the furthest thing from anyone's mind.

We were lucky in Erie County; the storm barely brushed us. Days of preparation resulted in no real response in our area, though we did send a swift water rescue team, incident management team, and other emergency personnel from our county downstate to help in the storm recovery. The preparation for the storm did help in 2014, when the county was struck by blizzards in January and March and Winter Storm Knife in November. We learned from preparing for Sandy and took advantage of that knowledge later.

I knew it would be some time before the State team would address the Bills lease again. In early November, we worked with various State departments and agencies on a number of matters related to the storm, including even offering and working with the State to address the housing needs of those dislocated from their homes because of the storm. Howard deeply appreciated our efforts, writing back upon reviewing our proposal: "county executive: extraordinary effort—very helpful. I am looping in our housing commissioner Darryl Towns, and head of DHSES (Department of Homeland Security and Emergency Services). Hg."

I checked in with the governor, Howard, and Joe every now and then just to offer anything we could, but also to tell them the extraordinary job they were doing to address a true disaster. In a time of great need, they showed incredible leadership skills and should be remembered for their efforts.

With the State preoccupied with Sandy, we worked with the Bills to resolve some of the minor issues outstanding. Rich talked to Jeff about the one-year extension and how it was unnecessary at this point. Liz Burakowski and Mike Siragusa worked on a few matters related to timing of construction and how much the County would have to borrow annually. On November 9, Rich sent Leecia Eve an email offering to catch up on a number of matters, including the Bills lease. We figured Leecia would be a good starting point to get the State involved again, as she could broach the subject when appropriate with Howard.

Rich and Leecia spoke on Sunday, November 11, for about forty-five minutes on Bills and Sandy issues. Based on Rich's email notes of the phone conference he sent to me on November 13, she indicated Howard and she had casually discussed how they needed to conclude the Bills lease, and looked forward to the day when they could focus on it as their storm-related duties eased up. Rich tried to see if completing the agreement by Thanksgiving was possible. She thought it might be, and said she would bring it up with Howard later that day. Rich also told her Howard never did get back to me on the operating split contributions, though we understood why.

While the conversation might not have been much, it was at least something and started the parties back down the path to getting a lease signed. Things were returning to normal, and the Bills were hosting the rival Miami Dolphins on a nationally televised Thursday night game. We all felt good about the direction we were heading.

I don't remember if the Bills won the game against the Dolphins, but I do recall one event from the night. Night games are always tough on security because patrons to the game are usually a different breed—younger, rowdier, and more exuberant—compared to day games, and often are more intoxicated. There are always more people ejected from night games than day games, and this game was no different. There were four times as many calls for ambulance service and many more ejections compared to a day game.

Unfortunately, one patron was ejected from the stadium that night and was never seen alive again by his game-day party. David Gerken, Jr., a Rochester-area Dolphins fan, somehow fell into Smokes Creek behind the stadium and died from either drowning or hypothermia. I learned of his death on Friday morning when emergency crews were still searching for him. There were times when Rich and I felt like the lease negotiations were going nowhere, but we never felt as disconsolate as we did upon hearing the news of Mr. Gerken's death. People go to football games to enjoy themselves and have a great time watching their team. No one goes thinking death might result.

I ordered our department of emergency services to work with the sheriff's office to piece together a timeline of events to try to figure out what had occurred. I also had staff contact the Bills to learn what, if anything, they knew about his ejection and subsequent death.

I was interviewed that afternoon at the dedication of a new name for a park, where I expressed my condolences to David Gerken's family and stressed that people attending the games needed to act more civilly, drink less alcohol, and just enjoy the game-day experience in a safe manner. I was asked about the lease but refrained from discussing it, instead focusing on Mr. Gerken's death and how I'd already taken action to find out what had happened.

Eventually we learned that Mr. Gerken was ejected from the stadium for violating the fan code of conduct instituted for all games. Based on published reports, his brother offered to leave the stadium with him, but he told his brother to go back in and enjoy the game and he would be at a nearby bar. He in fact went to the nearby bar but eventually left, only to be found by his father the following day deceased in Smokes Creek.

When I look back on the lease negotiations, it is this incident that is the saddest of all. No one should go to a football game with family and friends and end up dead the next day. The incident also had an effect on the county and the Bills. We made it a priority to increase security and change the ways individuals are handled by security and our sheriff's office. A new fence was installed between the perimeter of the stadium property and Smokes Creek, and many more security officials and sheriff's deputies would be added to the facility on game days. While some things are unavoidable, all involved in our discussions made sure the security of the facility and game-day patrons were always discussed and addressed, and it was the death of Mr. Gerken that reinforced this point.

Chapter 20

In the Red Zone

At the conclusion of the Detroit meeting, all parties knew we were close but had not yet reached a comprehensive deal. We had reached what every football fan knows as the "red zone." We were within twenty yards of the end zone, with the goal line in sight, but we had not crossed it yet. Our task now was to cross the goal line and score the touchdown, not settle for the equivalent of a field goal by entering a one-year extension of the current lease, or worse, not getting a deal done before Mr. Wilson passed away, which would have been the equivalent of a huge game-ending turnover.

After Sandy struck, Rich Tobe kept up the lines of communication with Leecia Eve and Irwin Raij, while I spoke to Lt. Governor Bob Duffy and his chief of staff John Maggiore. We were told information was being shared with Howard Glaser, and as soon as he felt he could dedicate time to the lease negotiations, we would hear from him again. I did not want to push Howard at this time, knowing he still had his hands full with the response to Sandy, but we all knew the time would be right to recommence the talks soon.

The process sped up when on Monday, November 19, I put in a call to Howard, and Rich sent him an email, to let him know Jeff Littmann had contacted Rich with news about the NFL's position on the lease. The team felt the time was right to get back to the bargaining table. I was told Howard was unavailable and that he would call me back later in the day. About an hour later, I received a call from Howard in which he said he had just finished a forty-five-minute discussion with Jeff, and he agreed the time was right to pick up where we had left off.

Jeff had told Howard that the Bills wanted to go straight to drafting a lease, but Howard told me now he wasn't sure that was the best plan, although he'd been pushing for it before. I told him that Rich, Irwin, and I all agreed it made sense to draft a memorandum of understanding between the parties and get that signed, which we could release to the media, as we were not going to get final agreements any time soon. In a normal business transaction, a memorandum of understanding—or "MOU," as we call it—would be signed between parties detailing all the major terms agreed to by the parties before the final documents were drafted. It was something my County team, as well as Irwin, had discussed as the next plausible step for the negotiations to take, but which Howard previously had not seemed interested in taking.

The benefit of having a MOU was that we could negotiate all the major terms, sign off on them, and announce the deal publicly, as well as take it to the NFL for its approval, and then finalize all the minor issues that would otherwise hold up signing a lease to a much later date. I think mentioning that we could get a MOU done much quicker than a final lease and all the ancillary documents, and announce that to the media, sealed the deal with Howard. By the end of the discussion, he agreed we should seek to get a MOU signed and let the attorneys hash out the final details.

I was glad to hear that Howard had now accepted the premise of entering into a MOU, instead of his prior position of trying to conclude the transaction by getting all documents completed and signed as soon as possible. I believe after the response to Sandy subsided, Howard reflected on the complexity of the transaction—the numerous details still to be negotiated and the time it would take to do so—and decided it would be better to lock in the major terms between the key parties and let the lawyers negotiate the rest. In effect, Howard had "seen the light" on the issues still to be resolved; now that he was not insisting on the immediate closing of the transaction, I felt we could expect a much smoother discussion.

Howard also told me that Irwin had the State's outside counsel prepare a rough draft of a MOU in October, and he would release the working copy of the MOU no later than the following day to us.

He asked us to review it and send our comments back to him. Then when we were all in agreement, he would send the MOU to the Bills.

I reminded Howard we still had to resolve the cost-sharing portion as it pertained to the operating and working capital to be provided to the Bills by the State and the County. Howard had previously pushed for a fifty-fifty percent split of future operating costs, while I had argued for a 57 to 43 percent split of costs. Howard rejected my proposal, though he did say to come back with an offer and he would review it. I remember not being happy with his rejection, but said I would get back to him after we had a chance to review the MOU.

The following day, November 20, Rich, Irwin, and I all received an email from Howard containing a marked-up version of the MOU between the Buffalo Bills, Inc., Erie County Stadium Corporation, and the County of Erie. The original version had been prepared by the State's counsel on October 20 (just prior to Sandy striking and based on a term sheet Jeff Littmann's office had prepared and emailed to the parties on October 13, following the Detroit meeting) but had never been shared with the working group. It was apparent Howard had made substantive changes to the document on November 20, as it was in a "marks on" tracked format version, and I could see from the document history that he'd significantly altered the content right before he emailed it to us. I concluded he had not actually looked at the draft MOU until that day, which made sense considering that until then he had been working under the premise that we would go straight from concluding the negotiations to signing final lease documents.

Reviewing the proposed MOU, I saw that while many of the major topics had been addressed, including Howard adding a clause requiring a separate non-relocation agreement be part of the final deal, a number of key issues still needed to be added to the MOU, including the State–County split and construction details. I forwarded the email and MOU to the rest of my team and sent Howard an email back thanking him for the document and letting him know we would get back to him soon with our comments.

It was imperative that my team and I resolved most of our issues with the State prior to the MOU being sent to the Bills negotiating team for their review and comment. As such, at 9 a.m. on November 21, I held a phone conference with the members of the County's team to go over the draft MOU. In addition to Rich and I, Liz Burakowski and Mike Siragusa from my office attended in person, while Chris Melvin, Martha Anderson, and Liz Columbo from Nixon Peabody attended by phone.

I began the conversation by talking about the recent developments, my phone conversation with Howard on November 19, and how the State had moved to now supporting a MOU. We then went line by line through the draft MOU, commenting on the terms and noting where revisions needed to be made. It was a long phone conversation because we felt many revisions were required. We agreed that the attorneys at Nixon Peabody would compile all of our comments and mark up the latest version to send back to the State. It was also agreed that I would call Howard and try to get him to once again look at the fairness of the split between State and County.

It was the day before Thanksgiving. Many people in my office were leaving work early to get ready for the next day's festivities, but everyone working on the lease negotiations knew we'd be there a while. Martha Anderson agreed to compile all comments from our team and prepare a revised document to go out for everyone's review later that day. That is exactly what she did, sending a revised version of the MOU, now marked with our revisions, to the County's team after 3 o'clock that afternoon.

After getting off the conference call around noon, I called Howard on his cell but did not get through to him. I let him know we were working on the MOU and should have a draft to him by the beginning of the following week at the latest. I also said I wanted to discuss further the split between the County and State for future operating expenses and looked forward to his return call. Finally, after the past month he'd had, I wished him and his family a very happy and relaxing Thanksgiving. I also made a call to the governor and left him a message wishing him the same for Thanksgiving. The governor sent me a text later that evening wishing me the same and thanking our team in Erie County for sending help downstate during Sandy.

I had not heard back from Howard on Friday or Saturday. So, on Saturday, November 24, I sent him an email to see if he got my message and asking him to call me on my cell phone when he had the chance. While I dealt with Howard, Rich had a cordial conversation with Jeff Littmann, letting him know what was happening on the County's end and to resolve a few issues the County and the team had that did not require the State's involvement. Throughout the weekend, Martha kept revising the MOU, and on Monday morning she sent the revised version to Irwin, noting it still needed to be reviewed by the rest of the County team, and hence was subject to further revision. Rich, Mike Siragusa, and I reviewed the document on Monday, and with no further revisions from us, Rich forwarded the revised MOU to Howard and Leecia Eve. Howard acknowledged receiving it, and then we heard nothing until late on Wednesday, November 28, when he sent a further revised version back to us for our review. Then Howard and Rich talked, at which time Howard let him know he was talking to Jeff.

If all this sounds monotonous and tedious, it isn't in reality. For those not accustomed to the method in which business transactions are closed, the slow, back-and-forth process I have described is typical prior to a deal being reached. In football parlance, we were slowly advancing upfield by grinding out a few yards at a time. There would be no pass reception to the corner of the end zone to end this drive. It would be a slow slog of gaining ground a couple of yards at a time.

The ground game continued for the next few days, with phone calls going back and forth, culminating with the County's and the State's teams seeming to agree on the vast majority of language for the MOU (but still not the split for future expenses). Howard then sent a revised version of the document to Jeff and Rich on the morning of Tuesday December 4, 2012. Upon reading the version Howard sent, we realized some problems existed.

First, and most important, the MOU no longer had the strong separate non-relocation agreement language in it. Without a separate non-relocation agreement, we would not have a deal. We found out afterward that the change was due to Jeff's prodding Howard to remove the direct language regarding the non-relocation agreement and replace it with more nebulous terms. This was not acceptable to me.

Second, a question remained as to the length of the agreement being either a seven- or ten-year term. While the MOU spoke of a ten-year term, other terms therein made it sound like a seven-year term, which the Bills would just buy out. While we would have protection through injunctive relief and a liquidated damages clause for payment of $400 million dollars if the team attempted to leave during the first seven years, afterward it was questionable what right the County and State had to ensure the Bills would stay. There was no question the team could pay a $28,363,500 termination clause on the seventh anniversary of the lease, but what happened after if the team stayed? It could be interpreted that if the team waited until the eighth year, they could possibly leave without paying any fee. Thus, this term had to be strengthened to protect the community in the event the team did not exercise the termination clause after the seventh year.

Meanwhile, and tangential to the lease negotiations, on December 4, 2012, by a slim one-vote majority, the Erie County Legislature passed its version of the 2013 budget, which cut more than $8 million from my original proposal. If the cuts were substantive in nature (jobs, nonmandated programs, etc.), it would have been acceptable, but the legislature "cut" in areas in which we were required by law to spend. Under Erie County's Charter, I could veto additions but not cuts, so I was stuck with them. In effect, the Legislature made phony cuts, thereby rendering the budget technically in balance but in reality out of balance. It meant my budget staff and I would have to implement numerous cost-control measures to ensure the budget balanced by the end of the fiscal year, including withholding spending in areas that were legally approved.

How did this affect the lease negotiations? Because it meant we had no choice but to ensure that the County's share of the split of future operating spending was at or below 43 percent. We simply would not have the money to pay for a fifty-fifty split.

As such, Rich sent Howard an email on the morning of December 5, noting our substantive issues with the MOU and the problem we now had because of the budget the legislature had passed. Howard responded about fifteen minutes later, agreeing we needed to clarify the language regarding the lease term and that they were running numbers regarding the future operating subsidy. Reading this email, I felt we were very close to an agreement.

But at 5:13 that evening, Rich and Howard received an email from Jeff Littmann, which Rich immediately forwarded to me. Upon reading it, I felt we had been sacked back at the thirty-five-yard line. We had been at the five-yard-line, ready to score. Now we were no longer in the red zone.

Chapter 21

They Might as Well Go Now
If That Is the Case

Jeff's December 5th email immediately confirmed for us what we had
assumed: Jeff and Howard had been communicating behind the scenes.
This was not in itself an issue, as the parties often talked even if nothing
was substantively happening. However, it appeared that Jeff was under
the assumption that certain actions were going to take place, and more
important, that a separate non-relocation would not be included in the
final documents. Part of Jeff's December 5th email read:

> When we reached a consensus back on October 12th it
> was predicated upon the mutual understanding that the
> deal would be patterned off the 1998 documents with only
> those changes as are necessary to reflect the revised deal
> terms. The Non-Relocation Agreement (NRA), separate from
> the stadium lease, was not part of that understanding. The
> draft of the NRA sent to us reads like an acquisition of an
> interest in the franchise than an ancillary lease document. It
> contains many provisions that violated the NFL's Constitu-
> tion and Bylaws and have zero chance of being approved
> by the Owners. It contains provisions that continue to bind
> the franchise even if the public entities default under the
> terms of the stadium lease. We cannot, and will not, sign
> an MOU that refers to this NRA.

Jeff's email continued, noting they were willing to work out the details, including in-person meetings if needed in Buffalo the week of December 17, and that "[b]y December 21 we should either have an agreeable MOU or know that we are at an impasse. In the event we cannot agree on an MOU by December 21, we will not be able to continue negotiations on the ten-year extension until acceptable arrangements have been made for the 2013 season. Given where we are at on the calendar, the terms of a one-year extension will have to be on the calendar on the agenda the week of December 17 as well." Jeff ended his email with an olive branch, noting we had come a long way together to craft the next era at the "Ralph" and we should "get together and start walking down this path."

While I realized we were no longer in the red zone, I did not think the deal was in jeopardy. Our terms of a non-relocation agreement were certainly not acceptable to the Bills, but I felt confident Jeff's statement was part hyperbole. I knew the NFL had agreed to non-relocation agreements for other teams. While it might have been the first time the Bills would seek NFL approval for such an agreement, it would not be the first time the NFL had agreed to one. So I was not too worried about the odds of getting a deal done, though I was miffed because we had been so close to the goal line before this setback.

Howard responded to Jeff's email later that evening, eventually noting we could massage the language in the non-relocation agreement, but we would need a non-relocation agreement that could be legally effective. This was his way of saying what I and my County team had been arguing for months: that it needed to be a stand-alone agreement, separate from the main lease documents. It was important someone responded to Jeff's email immediately, and better it was Howard. Jeff would often call Rich to commiserate about Howard's negotiating tactics. Howard offering his own olive branch in the email said we were willing to work out our differences.

Rich sent an email that night to Jeff and Howard, stating we very much wanted to get a deal done before the end of the season and could meet at any time. Rich also offered to talk that night or the following day. At this point, we on the County's team needed to talk to the State so that we had all our ducks in a row. We could not be on different pages. We needed to make a strong, cohesive argument as to why a separate non-relocation agreement was required.

So, on Thursday, December 6, Rich called Howard and discussed the matter. Mike Siragusa and I sat at Rich's conference table and listened to the discussion, though neither of us added anything. It was clear from Howard's voice he wanted to get a deal done as soon as possible, though he realized that without the separate non-relocation agreement being part of the final documents we really would not have accomplished what we wanted: an ironclad requirement to keep the team in Buffalo. After agreeing on the direction to take—to continue to push for a separate, strong non-relocation agreement—Rich agreed to call Jeff the next day and try to talk through the non-relocation language. In the meantime, all counsel for the State and the County would talk in a conference call to get their affairs in order.

At this time, counsel realized they were not sure what version of the non-relocation agreement had been sent by Howard to Jeff. By this time the documents had gone through so many incarnations, no one was sure Howard had actually sent Jeff the latest version and not an earlier work in progress. Rich agreed to try to find out from Jeff which version of the non-relocation agreement he had read that had made him so upset.

On December 7, Rich and Jeff talked and discussed the next steps to take. Per his usual manner, Jeff agreed to send an email out to everyone stating what steps were to be taken and by whom. That is exactly what he did. He sent an email at 4:53 p.m. on December 7, noting the Bills would work on a new version of the MOU, Russ Brandon and Rich Tobe would continue to work on a game-day security plan (which became all the more important following the death of David Gerken, Jr.), and Eugene Driker and Mike Schiavone would continue to talk to Irwin about the non-relocation terms.

For the next three days, all parties were working on various elements of the deal. Rich, Howard, and I worked on issues related to cash disbursements required as part of the proposed construction schedule ($59.74 million in the first quarter of 2013 and $70.26 million in the fourth quarter of 2013) and the possibility that neither the State nor the County could afford it based on cash-flow issues. As former comptroller of the County, I was concerned that the county comptroller's office would criticize our structuring of the deal if it negatively impacted the County's cash flow (in other words, if we dedicated so much cash to pay for the renovation of the Ralph that the County did not have enough cash on hand to pay its other bills). This issue was resolved when the Bills agreed to front most of the first-year construction costs, with the State and County paying for the rest after we issued bonds for the project in mid-2013.

At this point we were waiting for the Bills to send to everyone their revisions to the MOU. We received this at 4:49 p.m. on December 10, when Jeff forwarded to Howard and Rich an email from Mike Schiavone that included as an attachment a clean version of an MOU, as well as a marked-up version compared to the draft sent to the Bills on November 30. Rich called to tell me the new MOU had been received, and he was sending it to me for review. I remember being out at an event and telling Rich I would look at it in the morning. He asked me to please do so first thing when I got to the office as there were "issues." He left it at that.

I got to my office on the morning of December 11 around 8:45 and started to review the new MOU version from the Bills. Rich was not kidding when he said there were issues. While most of the revisions were minor, one of them was major, and it did not take long to find it.

The draft MOU everyone was working off of was broken into sections identified by roman numerals. Roman numeral II of the November 30 version of the MOU the State and County prepared was entitled "Obligation of the Bills to Remain in Buffalo." The section as drafted by the County and State included the language regarding the non-relocation terms (injunctive relief to keep the team in the town, $400 million liquidated damages clause if they did leave, etc.).

Based on Jeff's prior comments, I had expected the Bills to revise the section, and it had been revised—but not as I expected. In fact, the section had been deleted and replaced with one short phrase: "To Be Discussed."

It is fair to say I was troubled by this development. In fact, I was livid. I remember springing out of my seat and walking down to Rich's office to discuss this unforeseen development. Rich was not there, and neither was Liz Burakowski, whose office is next to Rich's.

Not knowing when they would be coming into the office, I decided to type up an email to both, as well as Mike Siragusa, Chris Melvin, and Martha Anderson. I sent the following email at 9:11 am:

If the Bills refuse to sign a non-relocation agreement, there will be no deal.

I will also hold a press conference soon to state what the sticking point is. We are not going to invest tens of millions of dollars for them to leave in 2 years. They might as well go now if that is the case.

When I wrote the email I was probably venting more than anything, but make no mistake: I was angry. There was no way I could agree to invest more than $30 million on behalf of the County on the renovation project and then watch the team leave within a couple of years if and when a new owner bought the team. If we did not get a lease done by the end of the year, I would certainly be criticized, but I could not agree to a lease without the iron-clad protections we wanted. I knew we were at a critical juncture of the negotiations: either we were going to protect the team for the foreseeable future, possibly through the death of Mr. Wilson, or we were opening up the door to the team moving upon Mr. Wilson's death. There was no way I was going to be the man who negotiated away the team by accepting a bad deal.

Chapter 22

I Probably Just Lied to the Media

It is fair to say that at this point of the negotiations everyone was antsy and nerves were frayed. No one on any side wanted the 2012 football season to end with no deal in place. While final signed documents would not be completed until sometime in 2013, we needed to announce the parties had reached a deal on the major terms very soon.

As an attorney who practiced in the corporate and finance area, I can say with some authority that there are points in a negotiation when lawyers need to get out of the way and let the deal happen, and other times when they need to figure out how to resolve a stalemate and hook the big fish or cut bait. We were never going to cut bait in this transaction, so it was important the lawyers figured out a way to hook this fish.

So the Bills and lawyers representing the State and the County agreed to meet by teleconference on Wednesday, December 12, to try to resolve the major differences, which really came down to whether there would be a separate non-relocation agreement. None of the principals would be on the call—only the attorneys. This was important because each of the principals—myself, Rich Tobe, Lt. Governor Robert Duffy, Howard Glaser, Russ Brandon, and Jeff Littmann—had too much invested in the transaction from an emotional point of view by that point. It was important that others more detached from the end product could discuss the sticking points and try to come to a resolution. So everyone agreed that only the attorneys would participate in the call.

While I might not have participated in the call, the principals on the State's and County's teams did agree on one fact: we needed to control the starting point of the next day's discussions. The best way to do that was to control the document to be reviewed. So in anticipation of the meeting, our lawyers agreed on new terms to send to the Bills' negotiating team, and at 9:08 p.m. on Tuesday, December 11, Stephen Boyett of Foley and Lardner (Irwin's firm) sent by email the revised MOU to Eugene Driker and Michael Schiavone who were representing the Bills. This new version included the separate non-relocation agreement terms we previously sought, but which had been deleted by Jeff Littmann in the version he sent us on December 10.

The call was scheduled for 11 a.m. I talked to Rich in the morning, and we were like a couple of old-school, 1950s-era expectant fathers: there was not much either of us could do other than try to focus on something else and wait for what we hoped would be a good result. The call lasted more than two hours. This was not surprising, as there were quite a few items to resolve, though the big one regarding the need for a strong, separate non-relocation agreement dwarfed the rest.

At 2:28 p.m. on Wednesday, December 12, Martha Anderson of Nixon Peabody sent Rich and the other attorneys her notes from the call. There were eleven areas of discussion, ranging from who was responsible for cost overruns (in the end, the Bills), to the percentage of minority and women business enterprises to be used during the construction period, to the amount to place in a construction contingency account, and the final term being the "Non-Relo," as it was described in Martha's email.

While the Bills' attorneys did not agree to the concept of a separate agreement on the call, the phone conference turned out to be very fruitful because it gave both sets of attorneys the opportunity to explain their positions and find common ground. In the end, the Bills were worried if the State or County significantly breached the terms of the main lease, such as we reneged and made no payments toward the renovation, they would have limited avenues of recourse and be stuck in Buffalo at least for the next seven years in a half-completed stadium. Our counsel was given the opportunity to show why a separate agreement was needed, and to remind the Bills' counsel that separate non-relocation agreements had been agreed to by the NFL, most recently in the lease transactions entered into for the New York Jets, New York Giants, and San Francisco 49ers. Thus the argument that the NFL would not accept a stand-alone non-relocation agreement was without merit.

More than anything, by not having any of the principals on the call, the lawyers were able to coolly attack each outstanding issue under the view that we were going to complete a deal once we got through these "minor" issues. While they were not minor, they each needed to be resolved if a final agreement was to be reached. Reviewing Martha's notes, it was quite apparent that of the eleven outstanding issues, ten could be easily resolved in short order. It was the eleventh item on her list, the Non-Relo, that could derail everything.

Rich and I briefly talked about the issues and agreed there must be a way to address the concerns the team had while still resulting in a separate, enforceable non-relocation agreement being entered into by the parties. Rich called Martha Anderson and asked her team at Nixon Peabody to review, as best as they could, the non-relocation agreements entered into as part of the Jets, Giants, and 49ers deals to determine how the issue was resolved in each of those transactions. He then sent an email to Howard Glaser, noting the attorneys' conference call appeared to have been productive and we in the County were taking the lead to resolve the non-relocation stalemate. Another conference call between the parties' counsel was scheduled for Friday, December 14, so it was imperative we tried to resolve the non-relocation agreement stalemate, as all other terms were basically agreed upon, at least between the combined governments and the Bills. There still remained a disagreement between the County and the State regarding the split of future expenses, however.

Similar to the prior conference call, none of the principals participated on the December 14, 2012, conference call. It was attorneys only and meant to resolve the final issues identified as outstanding on the last call. Also similar to the last call, the State and County prepared a revised MOU and sent that to the Bills attorneys prior to the call. Unlike the last call, however, this time, *finally*, the Bills agreed a separate non-relocation agreement would be part of the deal. In exchange for the Bills agreeing to such a term, the State and County's attorneys agreed the non-relocation agreement would lapse in the event the Bills were able to get a court of law to break the lease agreement if the State or County breached the lease, but not in the case that the team, no matter who owned it, filed for bankruptcy.

And just like that we were back to breaking the goal line with the ultimate touchdown in sight: an agreement by the parties to the terms of a new ten-year lease agreement.

But we were not there yet. The attorneys had accomplished much, but a few items remained to be resolved, including the split of future costs to be borne by the State and County, as well as some outstanding security issues at the stadium. Additionally, pursuant to the attorneys' call on Friday, December 14, the team's outside counsel Mike Schiavone agreed to revise the non-relocation agreement based on discussions at the meeting. It seemed like a good idea at the time because we had been working off of our own draft non-relocation agreement for many weeks now, so giving the Bills the chance to make minor amendments now seemed reasonable.

Mike Schiavone sent his revised version to the State's and County's counsel on Sunday, December 16. Upon reviewing it, our legal team immediately realized we'd been sacked again—though this time only back to the ten-yard line. While the Bills may have agreed in principle to the existence of a non-relocation agreement, the terms inserted by Mike Schiavone rendered it useless from our view. The non-relocation agreement needed to survive a possible bankruptcy by the owner of the team. It could not be "executory" in nature, under legal parlance. Mike's revisions made the non-relocation agreement executory in nature, meaning it could be broken in a bankruptcy proceeding filed by the team's owner, and the team could move. This was unacceptable, and Mike knew it.

Suffice to say, I was not happy—and neither was anyone on the County or State's side. We had been very close to an agreement, but not anymore. While Rich, Howard, Jeff, Russ, and I were trying to button up a few final matters (again, MWBE standards to follow, security issues, and the split between the State and County), in an attempt to resolve the non-relocation issue the lawyers met again by conference call at 11 a.m. on the morning of Tuesday, December 18. Our report back was not good: the Bills attorneys were not going to agree to a change from what they had just proposed. Just as there are times when you need the principals to step aside and let the attorneys work out the details, there are times when the attorneys need to step back and let the principals close the deal. This was such a time.

I was scheduled to drive to Albany that night so I could attend the Regional Economic Awards presentation the next day. The awards were to be presided over by Governor Cuomo, so I knew I would get a chance to talk to him in person. Before I left for Albany, Rich and I discussed the matter and agreed we needed to get Howard on the same page with us so we could send a unified message to Jeff and Russ to ensure that when I talked to the governor he would not disagree with our negotiation strategy. Howard and Rich spoke and agreed on a strategy in which Rich would send Jeff an email requesting a phone conference later that night so we could resolve the issues. At 2:22 p.m. on Tuesday, December 18, Rich sent Jeff the following email (unedited) and copied Howard on it:

Jeff,

I have been briefed on the lawyers call that took place earlier today. It sounds like the lawyers are having trouble closing up some of our open issues. Although there may be some "lawyers" issues, it also sounds as if they are having difficulty implementing some of the business terms that we have agreed to.

I have spoken to Howard about this matter. We both believe that a call involving you, Howard and me, along with one lawyer from each side could move this matter forward to conclusion.

We recommend a call for tonight at 6:30 p.m. Please advise if this works for you. We will provide call-in instructions later today.

If we can talk tonight, I will prepare a list of what I think are open issues. If you could do the same, we might be able to wrap up the MOU and Non-Relocation Agreement quickly.

I think we are very close and we all hope that we can resolve the issues rapidly.

Please let me know if you can participate in a call tonight. Of course, if 6:30 tonight does not work, let us know what time will, hopefully later tonight.

Rich

Our intentions in having Rich send the draft was to let Jeff know we, the principals, could close this deal if we did not let the attorneys mess it up. We figured Jeff would agree with that sentiment. However, the response we received from Jeff was not what we expected. At 4:14 p.m. on that same day, Jeff forwarded to Rich and Howard, with no comment from Jeff, an email Mike Schiavone had just sent out to Irwin Raij and all the parties' attorneys at 4:09 p.m. Receiving the following forwarded email without comment from Jeff led me to believe this was the official statement from the team. The (again unedited) email stated the following:

Dear Irwin:

During our conference call this morning, you and your colleagues again emphasized that a paramount concern of the State and County was that the NRA (non-relocation agreement) not be deemed an "executory contract," in order to minimize or eliminate the possibility of the Bills seeking to avoid its provisions by voluntarily pursuing a bankruptcy proceeding. If that concern continues to be reflected in the drafts your group produces, then we see no point in spending time debating the various other differences (and there are quite a few, as we touched on briefly this morning) between our last draft and yours.

To the extent we seek to have the benefit of a cross-default provision between the new lease and the NRA, the latter may well be deemed executory. But, with all due respect, we think that worrying about the Bills using that fact to avoid the NRA in bankruptcy is well wide of the mark and frankly doesn't reflect who the Bills are and the commitments that they have made and are prepared to continue to make to the greater Buffalo area. As you well know, absent insolvency, bankruptcy can't be used as a vehicle to avoid executory contracts and even with insolvency, there is a good-faith requirement that the courts uniformly enforce. So, the possibility of the Bills seeking bankruptcy to avoid the NRA is highly remote. Even beyond that fact, the possibility that the NFL would permit the Bills to seek bankruptcy is non-existent. Our principals feel quite strongly that by insisting that the NRA not be an executory contract, the County and State are ignoring the initial basis for our negotiation: the format of the existing lease will apply, modified only as needed to account for today's financial terms. We are simply unwilling to proceed if this remains your clients' position.

In discussions with senior NFL personnel today, we were told that it is "highly problematic" that your most recent draft would be approved either by the League or by the owners. They further confirmed our view that comparing this relatively modest and short-term renovation to a 30-year billion-dollar construction of a new stadium is simply inappropriate insofar as the scope of an NRA is concerned. Finally, in response to our report of your concerns about the possible use of the Bankruptcy Court by the Bills to reject the NRA, the League's response was that such action would be against League policy and would not be supported by it.

In reflecting on our request that, while we try to regroup and work through this complex problem, a one-year extension be put in place, please consider the email that Jeff Littmann sent to Howard Glaser and Rich Tobe on December 5th (and then also copied to Jay Bauman at the NFL) a copy of which is attached below. Neither of them disputed Jeff's position that, if no deal is in place by this coming Friday, we must have that extension in order to proceed with negotiations. Importantly, in our discussion with the NFL executives today, they are in full agreement with our position.

Given this situation, we are not prepared to deal with the other troublesome parts of your latest draft. We first need assurance that your clients, like ours, recognize that there are risks inherent in this transaction for both sides and each side must be prepared to accept its share of them. Perfection from the legal point of view is not something that either party can hope to achieve and still make a sound and practical business deal.

We ask that you consider our request with your clients and that we get the necessary extension in place, following which we'll turn our attention to trying to work through our mutual concerns on the NRA.

Mike

I did not see this email immediately, as Rich forwarded it to me later that evening. Upon reading it, I knew what Mike Schiavone's intention was. In effect, Mike was telling us they were unwilling to agree to the terms we expected, terms we thought the team had agreed to the previous week. Moreover, by stating they were "unwilling to proceed" if we did not change our position, he was drawing a line in the sand. He knew we were unwilling to proceed if we did not get the non-relocation agreement we wanted, and now the Bills were stating the same thing unless we gave in to their terms.

Howard Glaser then leveled the next volley, or perhaps nuclear strike, when at 4:22 p.m. on December 18, eight minutes after Mike Schiavone's email and in direct response to it, he sent the following email (unedited) to Jeff and Rich:

Based on the misrepresentation of facts to which your attorneys seem prone, Rich and I are both concerned about a lack of good faith on the part of your lawyers.

We are obviously not in a good place on a major term, and an extension is out of the questions.

We have made our commitments and obligations clear, your attorneys will not reciprocate. They are now raising questions about provisions in the original lease which all had agreed were a basic carryover from the prior agreement.

The call tonight is to clarify whether your attorneys are simply incapable of memorializing an agreement that we are in concert on, or whether they are acting on your instructions to spike the deal for other reasons.

hg

Joe McMahon was driving me to Albany that day. With Joe driving, I took a call from Rich in which he let me know about the latest emails and that things were tenuous. However, Rich told me that Howard, Jeff, and counsel from each side were going to try to break the logjam by participating in a conference call at 6:30 p.m. later that night. He then told me to call or send him any additional thoughts I might have after I read the emails, which he then forwarded to me while we spoke.

After hanging up with Rich, I read the emails and then sent him an email from my phone at 5:42 p.m. to reiterate we were seeking the strong non-relocation agreement because of what "could occur with a future owner. Remind them we have already gone through such an issue with the Sabres and the near loss of them. Mike S. is taking this personal and it isn't." That was in effect what was happening. We truly believed Mr. Wilson would not move the team while he was alive, but we needed the protection a non-relocation agreement would provide against some future owner who might not have the Buffalo area's best interests at heart.

Most people do not realize that on many occasions the lease negotiations between the Bills, State, and County seemingly fell apart, only to be rescued at the last moment. The next email I received was from Rich at 8:38 p.m. that night (Tuesday, December 18) stating he had just got off the call with the Bills and the State and it appeared there was "an agreement on the business terms. There were no changes and our overarching deal remains intact." Rich went on to note that "Jeff agrees that we have the right to have an enforceable non-relocation agreement."

As I have said, sometimes attorneys help move the process along, and other times they hinder it. In this situation, Jeff overruled his attorneys. Rich's email noted that Mike Schiavone continued to argue against the need for a separate non-relocation agreement during the phone conference call; however, when the County and State agreed the team should have the right to leave if either the County or State committed a major default that we did not cure, Jeff said a separate, enforceable non-relocation agreement was acceptable. With that, after a day of ups and downs and threats and bluster, the issue of whether there would be a separate, strong non-relocation agreement was over: there would be one.

We had not yet crossed the goal line, however. That would require having a signed MOU in hand and announcing it to the world. We were not quite there yet because the final terms of the non-relocation agreement and MOU had to be agreed upon by all. Nevertheless, we were close, and I knew the status of the negotiations would be the subject of discussion tomorrow when I saw the governor at the awards presentation and following luncheon at the Governor's Mansion.

Each year, the Economic Development Councils representing each region of our state compete for hundreds of millions of dollars in state awards. Each council submits a plan based on specific projects to be funded, and the State makes the final decision on the amount per region and projects to be funded. Every region knows it is going to be awarded something, but not how much and for what projects. The announcement in December of each year is the economic development equivalent of the Super Bowl. Hundreds of millions of dollars of state assistance, and the jobs that eventually result therefrom, are on the line.

The event was scheduled for 10 a.m. in Albany at the State Performing Arts Center at the Empire State Plaza, commonly known as the Egg. With the pageantry of an awards show, Governor Cuomo, Lt. Governor Duffy, Assembly Speaker Sheldon Silver, and Senate Leader Dean Skelos (the latter two since convicted of crimes and removed from office), as well as a slew of officials from across the state joined to find out how each region would fare. The event was emceed by CNBC's Maria Bartiromo, and every region had its moment in the sun: when each region was announced, everyone joined Ms. Bartiromo, the governor, and others on the stage to celebrate their award.

Prior to the beginning of the event, I spoke to Governor Cuomo for a few moments behind the scenes, and of course the topic was the Bills lease negotiation's status. I mentioned to the governor how it appeared we were very close to announcing a deal. He definitely knew we were close and said he wanted to make a big announcement at the stadium prior to the next home game. I told him there was only one home game left on the schedule for the year: December 30 against the New York Jets. That piqued his interest. He said he looked forward to announcing a deal then. I saw Howard Glaser nearby, and as the governor left to perform his duties, Howard came up to me and said we should talk more about things after the awards ceremony ended. With that, I left the holding area to take my seat, and the awards show began soon thereafter.

No one from the western New York Region expected our region to receive a top prize because in January of 2012, at the State of the State Address, Governor Cuomo had announced the Buffalo Billion economic development award for our region. In effect, we had already won the competition by getting a commitment for a billion dollars from the State, so when it was announced that the WNY region was awarded $52.8 million for fifty-eight projects that day, one of the lower dollar amounts for awards, everyone in our group was very happy. I was certainly not going to complain about "only" winning $52.8 million after we had already received a billion-dollar commitment. With the announcement by Ms. Bartiromo, I joined my fellow WNY Economic Development Council members on stage for the smiling photo-op with the governor, Ms. Bartiromo, and others. I remember thanking the governor for the generous award on top of the Buffalo Billion, as well as telling the governor, "We have one more big announcement to make soon," to which he responded, "We certainly do."

After the ceremony, I headed outside the auditorium, did a couple of interviews with media about the award, and then spoke with Howard off to the side of the Egg's main entrance hallway. We talked about the negotiation's status but really focused on the split between the County and State. The total amount to be paid out in future years by the combined governments had been agreed upon with the Bills, but not the final split between the two governments. I reiterated the impact the tax cap had on the County's ability to pay a higher amount, and how with the limitations on revenue growth put in place by the State, Erie County could not afford to take a greater share of future expenses at this time.

Howard asked me if I would be willing to accept a fifty-fifty split during the final years for future operating expenses if the County paid significantly less than the State during the first years of the new lease. I said that might be agreeable and asked him to send me his proposal on the split with corresponding spreadsheets noting the amount to be spent per year so I could review things with my budget staff. He said he would do so very soon, and with that we concluded our conversation.

I did not realize it while we were talking, but off to the side was Tom Precious of *The Buffalo News*. Tom covers the New York State beat for *The Buffalo News* in Albany. I do not believe Tom heard anything Howard and I spoke about, but he definitely did see us speaking. Tom then asked me if we could talk about the Regional Economic Development Council Awards and the Bills lease. It was approximately noon, and I was leaving to go to the Governor's Mansion for a post-awards ceremony luncheon, so I told Tom I would take a quick couple of questions. I think I answered one question on the $52.8 million award, and then he asked me about the Bills lease negotiations. He told me his sources indicated some very intense discussions had occurred between the parties the previous day, and a deal appeared imminent.

At the time, I was a little surprised that he knew about the discussions, considering no more than twenty-four hours had passed since, but Albany is a place where secrets do not remain secrets for long. Unlike prior times when I refused to comment on whether meetings or discussions took place, this time I did not deny it. I noted significant talks had taken place in recent days, including the previous night, and while I would not say a deal was imminent, I did say that we had made a lot of progress in recent days and that I liked the position we were in. I went on to highlight the productive discussions we had had with the Bills and the State. Tom asked if we were we talking with any other parties about a long-term Bills lease—that is, a potential new owner. I said categorically *no*, which was true, and noted how we were all working very hard to wrap up a long-term lease.

With that, I left for Governor Cuomo's reception at the Governor's Mansion. The Mansion was decorated beautifully for the upcoming Christmas holiday. Unlike my visit to the Mansion in December 2011, people did not queue up to see the governor, as he walked around and mingled with all the guests. It was obvious he was happy about the awards ceremony and in very good spirits for the holiday. I briefly spoke to the governor again, thanked him for the Buffalo Billion and today's award, wished him a Merry Christmas, and then left with Joe McMahon to begin the long drive west from Albany to Buffalo.

I do not think we had reached Utica when I got a call from my press secretary Peter Anderson informing me that *The Buffalo News* website had just posted a Tom Precious story about the Bills lease negotiations and that I was quoted in the story. Peter said he would forward the story to me by email and if there were any inaccuracies I should let him know. Hanging up with Peter, I then read the story on my phone and called Peter back to let him know it was accurate as written. Peter said in the ten minutes or so since we'd last talked he'd been inundated by other local media who wanted to interview me about the story, especially the local television stations.

I generally loathe the long drive between Buffalo and Albany. But sometimes a long drive can be a good thing. This was one of those times. I knew I would not be back in Buffalo until after 7 p.m., meaning there was no way I would be back in time to be interviewed on camera for the 6 p.m. newscasts. I told Peter to let the media know I would not be available for any more interviews that day because I was traveling and did not expect to get back home until late in the day. So on this matter, Tom Precious wrote an exclusive for *The Buffalo News* that every other media outlet would have to quote from, which is exactly what they all did, as none of them would dare ignore such a story.

While the drive back might have been monotonous, it was not without work. A new version of the MOU and non-relocation agreement was circulated between the parties at 3:14 p.m. by Howard. Reviewing such a complicated document on a phone is not easy, but after reading it over, I emailed Rich and our attorneys at 3:39 p.m. to say it looked fine to me. I also noted that while I had not yet reviewed the non-relocation agreement, "[a]ssuming it is fine with counsel, I probably just lied to the media when I said a deal 'isn't imminent.' We might have a deal." I also mentioned that Governor Cuomo really wanted to announce the deal in conjunction with the last home game against the Jets.

The rest of the trip consisted of me talking to Rich and reading emails from all the parties. Drafts and redrafts of the MOU and non-relocation agreement were flying back and forth among parties. All involved agreed a final conference call needed to be held that night to try to wrap up all the details, but no one could agree on a time. At just about the time Joe and I arrived back in Buffalo, Rich sent the following email to every party's negotiating team:

> We were **not** able to get the lawyers together until late tonight, so we have decided rather to have them speak tomorrow morning as per below. The "principals" Jeff, Rich, and Howard should call in tomorrow at around 10:00 a.m. Please advise if this works. Call-in information will be supplied tomorrow. Rich (emphasis in original).

While everyone else might have been willing to call it a night, Howard was not. At 7:34 p.m., Howard sent an email to Rich, Jeff, a few others, and me that got right to the point. He said, "I don't care how late we go tonight [but] we should finish tonight. Our team is ready to work all night. My window to get this done is now."

Howard was right. We were so close, and if we could get it done now, we might as well do so. While Governor Cuomo wanted to close the deal so we could make a big announcement in conjunction with the Jets game on December 30, Howard wanted to close it immediately. After all the fits and starts we had getting the State to the table, if we had an agreement, we might as well seal the deal, sign the MOU, and announce it.

However, no level of pleading by Howard or anyone else could change the fact that certain key personnel were unable to participate in the conference call. Jeff could not locate Eugene Driker, and other attorneys for the County and State were unavailable as well. So at 10:48 p.m., even Howard had to admit no further discussions would be held that night. He sent an email out noting we were done for the day and should talk in the morning.

In the span of a week, the parties had gone from being close to sealing a deal, to having it fall apart, to being close again, to being sacked, and now finally being ready to cross the goal line. When I went to bed on the night of Wednesday, December 19, I realized after months of negotiations there was a very good chance we would be announcing in the next few days that we had come to terms on a lease agreement. Moreover, it was an iron-clad agreement that guaranteed the Bills would remain the *Buffalo* Bills for years to come.

Chapter 23

Touchdown

Waking up on Thursday, December 20, 2012, I felt this was going to be *the* day—the day we completed the terms of negotiation—the day on which all the effort we put in during the previous year finally came to fruition. I'm sure I bounded out of bed that morning and got to work earlier than usual. While I may have been excited to wrap up the deal, there was still work to be done, and the discussions now were between the State and the County, not the Bills.

I had spoken to our budget director, Bob Keating, many times throughout the negotiations and relied on his financial analysis and spreadsheets to guide what the County could afford. Rich and I knew that getting a lease done was paramount, but it could not be one that broke our proverbial piggy bank. We had to know the impact the lease would have on our bottom line.

Bob always provided us the details we needed, especially when it came to dealing with the State. The spreadsheets he provided us on Thursday, December 20, showed us that the difference from what we were seeking and what the State wanted was approximately $1.8 million per year through the term of the lease. While this was not a huge amount annually, it would strain our budget and cost the County nearly $20 million in the long run, which I knew would put me behind the eight ball in preparing future budgets.

When I said I could not afford a fifty-fifty percentage split with the State in the early years of the lease, it was as much a matter of fundamental fairness as it was based on Bob's financial analysis. If New York State continued to play such a key role in the lease arrangement, I believed it should pay a greater cost of the transaction, as we would inevitably have other costs associated with game-day operations that could not be foreseen.

I called Howard Glaser on the morning of December 20 to see where he was in providing his new County–State spending split proposal. I didn't reach him but left a detailed message. Around lunch time, Rich Tobe told me he had spoken to Howard, who had said we would get his latest counterproposal by late afternoon. I think I rolled my eyes hearing this because by then the press offices for the County, team, and State were coordinating efforts to hold a press conference the next morning announcing that a MOU on a new lease had been reached.

I would have been fine with waiting until the following week to hold the press conference, or even later in the day on Friday, December 21, but the governor wanted to do it right away. Moreover, he really wanted to announce it the next morning because a winter storm was expected to hit Buffalo mid-afternoon, and he did not want to fly into it. My press team had originally scheduled a photo shoot with Jim Fink of Buffalo Business First at the Ralph on the morning of December 21 for a story Jim was writing on the status of the negotiations, so I certainly could do it. I told my press secretary Peter Anderson to tell Jim I would not be able to attend the photo shoot but not to tell him why, as he would learn the reason soon enough.

So while our press teams started to work on a unified message to send, I was still waiting for Howard's split proposal. Theoretically, we could announce that a deal had been reached between the Bills, the County, and the State without the split being agreed on yet, but it would have looked ridiculous to the media if they asked why it was still unknown at this point how much the State and County would pay in future years. It needed to get done.

Late that afternoon, Peter Anderson walked into my office and told me that someone from the State's press office, unbeknownst to the press teams for the County and the Bills, had spoken to Tom Precious of *The Buffalo News* and informed them a deal had been reached and would be announced the next morning, with Governor Cuomo flying in to Buffalo to announce the terms. However, unlike in most situations,

The Buffalo News had been provided this information only if it agreed not to release the story until much later in the night, so as not to tip off other media and to have an "exclusive" story in the morning's paper. Peter told me that another reporter at *The Buffalo News* called to get confirmation of Tom's story from the County.

At this time, we were still not sure if Tom Precious actually knew a deal had been reached, or if he was just fishing for a story based on rumors. I asked Peter to call Tom and find out what he knew about the proposed new lease's terms. I told Peter that if Tom knew the new terms, then Peter should confirm the deal under the same terms as allegedly given to the State: it was not to be released yet. If Tom did not know the new terms, then Peter should say nothing.

Finally, around 6:30 p.m., Howard sent to Rich his latest proposal regarding the County and the State's split of future operating and capital expenses. The renovation costs for the stadium remained the same: the Bills would pay 27.27 percent of the renovation, the State 41.45 percent, and the County 31.27 percent. Thus, the County would be paying 43 percent of the public's share, while New York State would pay 57 percent.

Howard's proposal for future operating and infrastructure costs took into account the issues I identified but also addressed his concerns. He always thought the County and the State should pay equal amounts in regards to future operating and capital accounts, while I always argued the County was constrained by the tax cap and could not afford more at this time. His latest proposal split the baby down the middle, as he had suggested during our discussion in Albany: the County and State would pay 43 percent and 57 percent, respectively, in the first year of the lease, and then the split would change annually by 1 percent until, in 2020, the County and State would pay an equal amount. As a result, during the first year of the new lease, the County would pay $3.324 million in combined annual infrastructure capital, working capital, game-day, and annual operating subsidies, while the State would pay $4.407 million for the same items. Each year, the County's share would increase by one percentage point, and the State's share would decrease by one percent, such that in 2020 the State and County would both be paying $4.742 million.

This was a proposal I could accept without thinking twice. Because of how we structured the deal and how we negotiated with the State,

Erie County would pay less in 2013, the first year of the new lease, in combined annual infrastructure capital, working capital, game-day and annual operating subsidies than we were contracted to pay in 2012 under the old lease. In fact, in 2012, the County paid $7.332 million in relation to the Bills lease: $4.432 million for game-day and annual operating expenses and $2.9 million for our annual infrastructure maintenance commitment for the stadium.

In effect, because I had not given in to Howard's original proposals on the State–County split, I had saved the County $4 million in the first year. While the County did agree to pay for the one-time $40 million renovation price tag, this was basically offset by the drastic reduction in the annual operating expense; if that expense had continued to grow at the same rate under the 1998 lease terms, it would have quickly risen to more than $10 million a year. Thus, Howard's new proposal looked great for the County in both the short term and long term.

Although it was after 7 p.m., my office remained busy preparing for the next day's events. I showed Bob Keating the proposed spreadsheet, and he immediately smiled. He knew not only that it was eminently affordable but that it would reduce our costs over time. As such, I called Rich (he had left by now) to let him know the latest proposal was acceptable to us, and he reported back the same to Howard.

And just like that, we were done. Before I left the office, I called my father to ask him if he had any plans the next morning, other than his usual coffee klatch with his friends at the McDonalds in Lackawanna. He said only the cup of coffee or two with his friends was on his schedule. I told him to cancel it and that I would pick him up in the morning around 9 to join me at a press conference to announce we had a deal for a new Bills lease. I sensed the excitement in my dad's voice as he said he would love to be there.

I then confirmed a few more minor items with Peter Anderson and left the office with a big smile on my face, knowing all the work of the previous twelve months would bear fruit the following morning—we would finally reach the end zone to score the game-winning touchdown.

Chapter 24

I Think I Made Jerry Sullivan Speechless

I normally don't need to set my alarm to wake up in the morning; I usually wake up around the same time each day. There was not much reason to worry about sleeping in on the morning of Friday, December 21, 2012, however, because I don't think I slept much at all the night before. But if I was tired from lack of sleep, I didn't feel it when I arrived at the office before 8.

Most of my staff doesn't arrive until after 8:30 each morning. On this day, the office was already buzzing with activity by the time I got there. It seemed everyone wanted to attend the announcement ceremony later that morning. Now the cat was out of the bag for the community, too: when I got in, I saw *The Buffalo News* sitting on my desk with its cover story noting a new lease deal had been reached and would be announced this morning at Ralph Wilson Stadium. My cell phone started blowing up with congratulatory calls and texts. There were so many I could not answer them all.

Before we gathered our troops and made the trip out to the Ralph, Peter Anderson said there appeared to be an issue with Governor Cuomo's attendance at the event—his plane had not yet left from the airport in Westchester County because of high winds there. His staff was frantically trying to delay the event until the afternoon, but he had wanted it to be held in the morning, and his staff had been contacting media all morning to let them know of the big announcement, so there was no pushing it back to later in the day. Considering the flight's duration was under an hour, I figured the governor would arrive by 10:30 at the latest, so I expected he would be there in time.

A caravan of cars left the Rath Building that morning—everyone who had played a role in the negotiations was going to attend the announcement. Joe McMahon drove Jennifer Hibit and I out in one vehicle, Rich Tobe was joined by Liz Burakowski and others in another car, and Peter Anderson headed out in a third vehicle with Mike Siragusa and others.

There was room for one more in my vehicle: my dad, whom we would pick up at my parents' house on Della Drive in Lackawanna. My parents live in the fourth ward of Lackawanna, which is the area adjacent to Hamburg and Orchard Park and includes Abbott Road. The drive from my parents' neighborhood off of Abbott Road to the Ralph is less than five minutes by car, and about twenty minutes by bike. I know the ride well because I sometimes rode my bike up to the Ralph, then known as Rich Stadium, back in the late '70s and early '80s.

When we pulled up to my parents' house, I could see my dad looking out the front window waiting for us to arrive. When we entered the house, my mom told me that dad was like a little kid waiting for his first friend to show up for his birthday party. Mom said he'd also called all his friends to let them know he would not make it to McDonalds' because he was attending the new lease deal announcement, so now he was acting like the big kid on the block. I laughed and said the next time he joined his friends they should buy his coffee.

Hopping in the car for the now very short trip to the Ralph, I kept thinking how what we announced today would affect the lives of many people like my dad and his friends. We were guaranteeing the Bills would be playing in Buffalo for the foreseeable future. For many years to come, Bills' fans everywhere would be talking about the team's play at coffee klatches, diners, clubs, and gatherings. No, it was not a perfect transaction—we would still have issues to deal with regarding the sale of the team upon Mr. Wilson's death—but no deal is ever perfect, and we were confident that this one would set the table for future success.

We pulled into the Ralph Wilson Stadium complex and went straight to the administration building. Entering the building, we were shepherded to an office near the back entrance to the building's media room. Peter Anderson was already there working with the Bills press relations director, Scott Berchtold, on getting the media situated before the announcement began. Peter also said something about "working on a video connection," but at that point I wasn't sure what he was referring to.

About five minutes after we reached the stadium complex, Robert Duffy arrived with his staff. Bob is a lifelong Bills' fan, so the announcement was a major accomplishment for him, and he deserved to be there because he played a key role in making the deal a reality. While the LG retained a smile on his face, I could tell when he started speaking that all was not well: the governor would not be attending the press conference. The LG said the conditions outside of New York City had grown worse, and it was just too unsafe to try to fly out from the Westchester airport. Thus, neither the governor nor Howard Glaser would be attending the announcement, though Peter Anderson and others were working frantically to patch the governor in by video feed. Now I understood what Peter was trying to tell me a few minutes earlier.

I was introducing my father to everyone when Russ Brandon walked into the room. Russ and I gave each other a big handshake and hug, and I said all we'd worked on for the past year was finally being realized with a good lease for the community and team. I asked Russ to relay my thanks to Mr. Wilson for negotiating in good faith and selling the deal to the rest of the NFL. We chatted a few minutes with Russ and Bills play-by-play announcer John Murphy, and then Scott and Peter walked into the room and said we were ready to begin. Scott went over the agenda for the press conference (speaking order, how the Q&A period would be handled, etc.), and then we headed out to face the teeming mass of media.

Every local media outlet had multiple reporters, cameramen, and photographers present. The room was packed to the hilt. Buffalo Mayor Byron Brown was present, as well as a number of State assemblymen and senators and Erie County legislators. I saw Rich Tobe and the other members of my staff standing off to the side of the room with huge smiles on their faces. When I walked out with Russ and the LG, my dad was alongside us. A reporter asked, "Who's that guy?" I didn't need to answer the question because "that guy" quickly introduced himself as Charlie Poloncarz to the group of reporters.

Scott took to the stage, set the parameters for the announcement, and then introduced the LG to say a few words at the podium. The podium we were using was not the traditional Bills podium but a big one with New York State's seal on it and a plaque on top bearing the words "Keeping the Bills in Buffalo." Since we'd expected the governor to be in attendance, the stage had been decked out accordingly.

After a few words of thanks, the LG turned the event over to Governor Andrew Cuomo, who was appearing through a video feed from downstate. The governor was seated alone at a table with a red, white, and blue Buffalo Bills hat on the table and an American and New York State flag behind him. Although he appeared pleased, I knew he was disappointed not to attend in person. Nevertheless, he thanked all who played a role in getting the deal done, including "a special thank you to Mr. Ralph Wilson for honoring his commitment to Buffalo and the people of western New York," and then he started to discuss the terms of the lease.

In doing so, the governor created a bit of a firestorm, as while everyone else had agreed beforehand to refer to a ten-year lease, he called it an "exciting agreement—the agreement basically commits the Bills to staying at Ralph Wilson Stadium for another seven years that will take us through 2020." The lease was a ten-year lease with a buyout after the seventh year. But because the governor had said "seven years," there would be many questions from the media and others on what the term of the lease actually was.

The governor then offered his opinion on the lease and his commitment to Buffalo, and announced he would "be signing now," and proceeded to sign an official-looking document. While it might have looked official, whatever the governor signed was certainly not the memorandum of understanding or the final lease. At that moment, I joked to Russ Brandon, "I think the governor just signed a proclamation declaring it Ralph Wilson Day in New York State."

In fact, the governor never needed to sign anything, as his signature was not required on any of our documents. Rather, Kenneth Adams, the president of the Empire State Development Corporation, needed to sign on behalf of the Erie County Stadium Corporation. In the end, I have no idea what Governor Cuomo signed, but he certainly looked official for the press pointing their cameras in his direction.

After the governor finished, LG Duffy once again took the stage and introduced Russ Brandon. Russ delivered a short speech thanking all who had played a role, and then was set to present the governor with a Buffalo Bills helmet, but since the governor was not present, he joked he would give the helmet to the LG instead to pass on to the governor, though he was "pretty sure it would not make it to his office." Russ then introduced me, and the first words I said at the podium were, "I'll be sure to give that helmet to Governor Cuomo, if you like," which drew a nice round of laughter.

I don't prepare a speech for every press conference I attend, but I definitely had one ready for this announcement, primarily to ensure I didn't forget anyone I wanted to thank, most importantly Governor Cuomo, Mr. Wilson, and all the members of our negotiating teams who had worked so hard for so long. I also wanted to highlight all we had done to get to this point, which I described as "an early Christmas gift for Bills fans everywhere across the world."

I noted how hard it was to get the deal done, stating there "were over fifty meetings, thousands of emails, countless of hours that got us to this point." I was sure to mention that this was a *ten-year* deal that also was forward thinking in requiring the parties to work together to come up with a long-term solution for the needs of the team. Moreover, I noted how this deal created "a more affordable capital plan" for the State and County to invest in the stadium complex, yet also "ensure[d] the structural integrity not only of State and County government but [also] the economic viability of the Bills here in western New York." I noted that what we were signing was an "agreement that ensures the Buffalo Bills continue to be the Buffalo Bills" and that "Bills fans across the globe would be watching the Buffalo Bills for years to come."

With that, I ended my speech, and Russ and LG Duffy joined me onstage to answer questions from the media. As I had anticipated, the media started by questioning the team's commitment to the region since at this point it really was not clear to them whether the lease was for seven or ten years. Someone asked Russ if the team's commitment was guaranteed for the fans, and he replied "guarantee."

I was then asked by Jim Fink of Buffalo Business First whether it was a seven- or ten-year lease. I said it was a ten-year lease, during the first seven years of which "it is locked in," and if the team tried to leave, "the County and State could demand specific performance, and if specific performance could not be obtained, then the organization would have to pay $400 million." I then noted that at the end of the seventh year the team would have an option to buy out the last three years of the lease for approximately $28 million, but that we were focused on the future by committing County, State, and team dollars for the potential to build a new stadium in years eight, nine, and ten of the lease agreement.

Rich Newberg of WIVB CBS 4 immediately said, "$29 million is not a lot of money." Although Rich had not aimed his question directly at me, I responded by informing everyone that the Bills could have left prior to the last year of the 1998 lease for $2 million, and that Mr. Wilson had shown his commitment to the area by not buying out the prior lease for what I described as "peanuts in the last few years." The LG and Russ then reiterated that the team chose to stay in the community even though they could have left for just a few million dollars during the recent past. The LG noted that the announcement was "like a cherry on top of a sundae" as it pertained to the investment the State was making and the positive news the region was starting to see.

After we had answered several more questions about the lease and the stadium asked in slightly different ways, Scott Brown of WGRZ NBC 2 asked Russ about Mr. Wilson's declining health and what type of "succession plans there are" for the team upon his passing. The subject of Mr. Wilson's inevitable death was always a touchy one for the team. Russ answered the question diplomatically by focusing on "the here and now" and mentioning that the question about Mr. Wilson's death was becoming "tiresome" and how "we should be here today to applaud him." We all then left the stage to a round of applause from some, though not all, in attendance.

The next few minutes were spent answering reporters' questions one on one, including my speaking to a gaggle of reporters on how the specific performance and $400 million penalty clause contained in the agreement actually worked. I remember *Buffalo News* reporter Jerry Sullivan trying to form a question on the penalty provision prohibiting the moving of the team, but not being able to get the question out. Jerry and I had played a round of golf over the summer, and I had told him then that we were going to demand a strong penalty clause. Back then, Jerry had said there was no way the Bills and the NFL would accept such a provision. Jerry is known for always having an opinion on a topic, but at this moment he seemed speechless. I don't think he could believe we were able to get such a strong provision in the lease.

Eventually, Jerry noted how in the summer we had talked about a penalty clause, and how he never thought we would get one in the agreement, but we did—how? I think I smiled and said it was all part of the negotiation process. We did not get everything we wanted, but we would not give up on that point. While I was talking with the media, my father joined me and was standing next to me. I introduced him to a number of reporters, including Jerry. As we walked away, my dad noted how Jerry didn't seem able to believe that we actually got the strong penalty clause in the lease. I laughed and said, "I think I made Jerry Sullivan speechless." Dad laughed and responded, "Impossible!"

After leaving the media room, I went back with Russ to his office so we could sign the actual memorandum of understanding. Peter Anderson and Scott Berchtold told us not to sign until they were ready with their cameras. Once we were given the go-ahead, we put pen to paper, and I joked that this time the signing was "for real," unlike whatever Governor Cuomo had signed earlier. We talked a few more minutes before I left to do an interview with Bills play-by-play man John Murphy for his nightly radio show.

I have known John for many years. He comes from a local political family and was previously a member of the Erie County Democratic Committee. He is married to Mary Travers Murphy, former Orchard Park Town Supervisor. John is a good man who cares about our community. He is also a true-blue Bills' fan and extremely grateful for the opportunity to call his favorite team's games.

During the interview, John and I talked about how it felt to have accomplished one of my stated goals as county executive and what it meant to the community to keep the team in Buffalo. I noted how the Bills are an integral part of our community, and the team is part "of our psyche." I told him that love for the team is generational, and that is one reason that I brought my father to the press conference. My dad had taken me to my first Bills game, against the Jets, and now I could repay him by keeping his team in our community and bringing him to today's event to witness it.

After the interview, as I left the administration building with my father and staff, I overheard Joe McMahon say, "Today is a good day."

Joe's usually right, but this time he got it wrong—it was not a good day, it was a *great* day. As we drove away from the stadium complex, my dad thanked me for bringing him. I told him it was the least I could do. We dropped him off back at the house, and as he left he said he would see me "later tonight."

At that point, a slight panic overtook me. With everything going on, I had forgotten I had scheduled a Christmas party at my house for friends and family that night, and I had purchased next to nothing. Thankfully, it was only around 1 p.m., and the first guest was not coming until 7, so after we returned to the office, I completed a few phone interviews related to the Bills announcement and then left to buy food and drink, clean the house, and prepare and host the party.

As you might expect, everyone at the party that evening was in the mood to celebrate. In fact, I think the party on the night of Friday, December 21, 2012, will go down in the annals of holiday parties as one for the ages—at least what I remember of it.

Chapter 25

The Legislative Interlude

With the Christmas holiday approaching, and the announcement of the MOU having been signed, everyone on my team decided to take a break on lease work. While we had announced a deal, we had not in fact signed a lease. A tremendous amount of work remained to be done to complete the transaction, including drafting all necessary documents related to the new lease. However, the vast majority of the remaining work would be completed by attorneys.

Rich and I agreed that following the New Year he would coordinate the efforts from the County's legal team and contact the State's team to get everyone on the same page as we moved forward. We also agreed I would handle the other part of the equation that needed to be completed soon: approval by the Erie County Legislature of the MOU.

Under Erie County's Charter, every County contract is subject to the approval of the County Legislature. While I might have announced the deal, and everyone assumed it was set in stone, if the Legislature rejected it, we would be back to square one. So, on Wednesday January 2, 2013, while Rich began coordinating the legal work, I started working with my team on getting the Legislature to approve the MOU as soon as possible. I brought together my chief of staff, Jennifer Hibit, legislative liaison Brian Bray, Mark Cornell and Peter Anderson of the communications team, and County attorney Mike Siragusa for a quick meeting on how we would strategize the process. While I did not think the Legislature would be so bold as to reject the deal, I figured they might try to amend it to look like they made a difference in the end product. There was no way we could allow this to happen, because if it did, the Bills, NFL, and State would look down harshly on the County for reneging on the terms agreed upon. While the Legislature might have a role pursuant to the County's charter, for all intents and purposes, their role was ministerial in nature: either approve or reject the transaction, but not amend it.

We also did not want to have to return to the Legislature at a later date to get its approval for every contract and agreement related to the MOU and final lease transaction. Therefore, Brian Bray worked with Mike Siragusa to draft the necessary document, "communication" in the Legislature's parlance, to transmit the now fully signed MOU to the Legislature, which would then cause the Legislature to begin its required actions. However, Brian and Mike drafted the communication in such a way that once the Legislature approved the MOU, it delegated to my office the power to draft and enter into every contract and side-agreement necessary to conclude the lease transaction. In effect, if the Legislature approved the communication with the resolution we proposed, we would never have to return to the Legislature for its approval of the transaction or any of the future lease documents unless we chose to do so. Brian then delivered the communication to the Legislature on January 3, where it was "clocked-in" by time stamp, thereby officially putting the Legislature on the clock.

The Legislature's first meeting for 2013 was scheduled on January 8. I did not expect the Legislature to approve the MOU at that meeting, but instead to assign it to a committee for deliberations. Assignments to committees are made by the Chairperson of the Legislature, so I spoke to Legislature Chairwoman Betty Jean Grant a day or two before their first meeting and asked her to assign it to the Economic Development Committee chaired by Legislator Thomas Loughran of Amherst. Legislator Loughran and I had been elected to County government in the fall of 2005 following the "Red-Green Fiscal Crisis" of 2004 and 2005. I knew Tom well, we have always been friends, and I figured he would give us a fair shake and shepherd the matter through without much problem. At the Legislature's January 8 meeting, Chairwoman Grant did what I asked of her when she assigned the matter to the Economic Development Committee.

The committee's meeting was scheduled for January 15. Prior to that meeting, I started calling and meeting with many of the legislators to discuss the proposal. Every time a legislator asked to amend the agreement, as I figured they would try, my answer was the same: no. Either they voted for or against the proposal, but they could not amend it. I knew they were all desperate to be part of the process, but if they amended the agreement, they could throw the whole set of negotiations into disarray.

While the legislators could not amend the agreement, that didn't mean they had no role. In fact, we did everything possible to make it look like the Legislature was an important party to the process in order to get their approval. Working with the Bills, we scheduled a tour of the facilities and a special presentation on the proposed renovation for January 17, and made sure members of the Bills' negotiating team were present for the committee hearing scheduled on January 15. We held multiple private meetings with legislators before the committee meeting so all knew what the terms were beforehand. We felt they were sufficiently advised of the terms of the MOU before the meeting.

However, I had also kept an ace up my sleeve that would become apparent at the committee meeting. Normally, a County executive doesn't appear before a meeting of the Legislature. While an executive might attend a session in the audience, such as when a certain constituent is being honored or for the first reorganization meeting after an election, a County executive never appears before the Legislature. That changed on February 15, when I walked into the Legislature's chambers and presented with Rich Tobe the administration's argument on why the MOU needed to be approved.

I could see the surprise on Legislators' faces. None of them expected me to be there. I think they were also surprised when the meeting started and I went into great detail on the terms of the agreement. I sincerely believe some of them thought I had no real role in the negotiations; that I was just a figurehead while Rich Tobe had done all the work. Some County executives are known for not really wanting to get involved in the nitty-gritty work that governing often amounts to. I am not that kind of County executive.

By showing up, I was subtly telling the legislators that this was one of the most important decisions they would make and that I expected them to vote yes. It was not just my appearance that made a difference; Russ Brandon led the team's contingent, and his appearance before the Legislature was the Bills' way of saying while we "respectfully request" your approval, we also expect it.

When the Legislature holds a committee meeting, usually only committee members show up, and typically not all of them. When I walked into the Legislature's chambers that morning, I saw every legislator in attendance. I was not surprised, as I expected every member to want to be seen as part of the discussion, though it meant it would be a long meeting as every member would probably speak.

True to my expectation, it was a long meeting. Committee chairman Tom Loughran opened with a few welcoming remarks on how important this meeting was, and then turned the discussion over to me. Rich and I began to go over the terms of the MOU. It was a fairly straightforward recitation of the deal. Then Russ Brandon discussed the deal from the team's point of view, basically reiterating that this transaction would ensure the team's viability for the future. The team was prepared to present a PowerPoint presentation on the proposal, but that was scrapped when the projector didn't work well in the brightly lighted room. After Russ finished his presentation, the legislators, one by one, peppered the assembled with question after question, all of which were fairly easy to respond to in a manner that satisfied the questioner. The legislators did their due diligence during the meeting, and we all expected them to approve the matter when it was sent back to the full body from the committee.

As we left the Legislature's chambers, we knew we had accomplished our mission of presenting a set of cogent reasons as to why the Legislature should approve the proposal. However, one additional action needed to be taken to get the Legislature on board: having them tour the stadium and see firsthand where the renovations would occur.

So, on January 17, I joined many County personnel and headed out to the Ralph to walk the site and watch a presentation by the Bills on the proposed project. It was a bright, sunny, cold day. We gathered at the team's administrative offices and then were led back to the team's teaching classroom. It looked pretty much like any classroom you would find on a college campus, and everyone took a seat and waited for the show to begin. Scanning the room, I could see all the legislators were in attendance, many of them looking like kids in a candy store. Because this was an actual off-site meeting of the Economic Development Committee, and New York's open meetings laws applied, members of the media were also in attendance. Judging by their faces, they were all happy to be there.

Russ opened the program and then turned things over to Coach Doug Marrone, who discussed the prior season and his goals for the following year. Coach Marrone also thanked the County and the State's team for their dedication and working hard to keep the team in western New York. Then Russ introduced Scott Radecic from Populous, who went through the schematics and drawings showing what the stadium would look like post-renovation.

This was the moment the legislators and media had been waiting for, as it was the first time any of them saw the drawings. Cameras were clicking, and notes of Scott's presentation were being furiously scribbled down by members of the media. I watched to see if the designs had changed from what we had seen earlier. Except for some color variations, the architectural renderings were basically the same.

After Scott finished his presentation, we left the classroom and began a tour of the Ralph Wilson Stadium complex to see exactly where the renovations would take place. Every spot where work would take place was walked and discussed, including the areas outside the stadium such as the training facility and the location for the new football operations building. The majority of the tour was in the stadium, from the locker rooms, to the media center, concession stands, bathrooms, and everywhere in between, culminating with us all being led down to the field. As we walked out to midfield and scanned the surroundings, the legislators were smiling like children on Christmas morning

I have to admit that it was very cool to be on the field. Legislator Terry McCraken and I were kicking ourselves for not bringing a football to toss around. Everyone was beaming, especially the legislators, so I asked a few from both sides of the aisle what they thought of the plans and the proposal. Everyone I talked to said they thought it was a good plan. I knew then we had succeeded in getting them to vote yes without trying to amend the proposal.

The proof of that finally came on Thursday, January 24, when the Legislature voted unanimously to release the plan from the Economic

Development Committee, without amendments, and to approve the proposed MOU and give my administration the power to draft the agreements and close the transaction. If announcing the transaction back in December had been like scoring a touchdown, this was like kicking the extra point.

Now, only one task remained in order to finalize the deal: complete the contracts and sign the final documents.

Chapter 26

Blue Tick Hounds

Following the Legislature's approval of the MOU, everything was now in the hands of the attorneys, who were negotiating the final terms of every document related to the new lease. This was not a minor matter. While many assume the County, State and team entered into one document, the lease, to consummate the transaction, in fact there were many documents that still needed to be negotiated and signed by the parties to close the transaction.

These agreements included the lease of the stadium, parking lots, and related premises from the County to the State, the sublease from the State to the team, the non-relocation agreement, the agreements that controlled the renovation's construction, minority- and women-owned business participation and labor force goal agreements, security agreements, the agreements that would bind the NFL to the terms we negotiated, and so on and so on. The process to complete these agreements would be tedious and take several weeks to accomplish, but everyone felt comfortable that we would be able to finalize the agreements in March because much work had been done on each agreement by the attorneys while we were negotiating the MOU. While it was not a formality, per se, I believed we were well on our way to completing the transaction, and I was glad not to have to think about the lease every day, as I had done in 2012.

Rich Tobe, Mike Siragusa, Martha Anderson, and Chris Melvin, as well as their staffs, started to really dig into the weeds of every document. With so many documents to be negotiated, certain ones were assigned to each member of the team to review. The attorneys at Nixon Peabody (Chris and Martha's firm) were responsible for most of the documents, but everyone had a role to play among the legal teams. The same could be said for the State's legal team, headed by Howard Glaser and Irwin Raij, and backed by the attorneys Irwin oversaw at Foley and Lardner, and for the Bills' attorneys, led by Jeff Littmann and Mike Schiavone. I am not sure how many attorneys were involved at any one time, but the number easily surpassed ten and might have reached fifteen among all parties.

Throughout the weeks of January and early February 2013, Rich provided me with regular reports that everyone was plodding along in efforts to tie up all loose ends and complete the transaction by March. He noted a number of sticking points in many of the documents, but the attorneys were working through them. Some of these issues were minor, while others were not as pertained to County and State.

For example, there were disputes regarding whether the County and State would have oversight regarding the use of budget surpluses and change orders (we must have had that oversight pursuant to State and local laws), disclosure and joinder rules regarding the NFL's relationship to the transaction (they had to agree to the terms, otherwise all of our work would have been for naught), and even whether the team needed to provide to the County "as-built" architectural renderings of the newly renovated facility upon completion (they did have to because the Ralph is publicly owned). As each day passed, the number of disputes seemed to grow, such that on February 27, Steven Boyett of Foley and Lardner circulated an email to the State's and County's teams that included two documents listing all of the outstanding issues and disagreements. He listed the top fifteen issues in the body of his email.

Rich sent me Boyett's email on the following morning, and we then discussed the status of the deal at that point. Rich noted much of the goodwill derived from reaching and announcing the MOU was lost, and attorneys on all sides were starting to analyze the transaction to death. In its current state, there was no way we were going to complete the transaction in March, and if some of the terms our attorneys were fighting for were not successfully resolved to our benefit, it would be difficult to close the transaction.

I had to let that sink in for a moment. Rich is not a man with a flair for the dramatic when describing things. He was a fairly no-nonsense guy when it came to reciting matters related to the Bills lease. I could tell from the look on his face that he was serious. In effect, Rich was saying if we did not change the tone and tenor of the negotiations, as well as resolve the outstanding issues to our benefit, we might not have a deal.

As an attorney myself, I know all attorneys attempt to vigorously argue on behalf of their client's interests. However, sometimes attorneys go too far. Sometimes they have to be told enough is enough—close the deal, don't destroy it.

Rich agreed to work with Howard and Jeff to try to get everyone back on the same page and resolve the differences. If that didn't work, then Russ, the LG, and I needed to meet, or talk via conference call, to try to work things out. Rich would let me know the following week how things was progressing, and if we would need to schedule a call or meeting.

Things really did not get any better the following week. Rich, Howard, and Jeff were able to resolve a few minor issues, but many still existed (the list was now up to thirty-one separate issues needing resolving) and no side appeared to be willing to budge. Although we had announced the MOU and negotiated the major terms the previous year, it looked as if the deal could still fall apart. Within the dozens of documents, there remained myriad issues that needed to be agreed on. I didn't realize it then, but it was nearly time to release the proverbial hounds in order to end this impasse.

On Friday, March 8, at 6:04 a.m., Jeff Littmann sent the following email to Rich and Howard in what must have been a last-ditch effort of desperation on his part to salvage the transaction:

Subject: Blue Tick Hounds

Howard & Rich,

This chase has gone on too long. If we do not bring it to closure soon the game may be lost.

Today we will be like a charging, baying, slobbering Blue Tick Hound on a hot trail after a very long chase. We are going to catch this critter or die trying.

I will have for you this AM the following:

Draft Funding Schedule.
Pre-Construction Work Schedule and Invoices.
Our Open Issues List.

Please get me your open issues list as well as any other items that you think we owe you or that needed to "fill in the blanks."

Jeff

Rich forwarded me the email at 7:30 that morning and added the sole question: "Do I get combat pay for having to put up with the below set of metaphors?" Reading Jeff's email, I chuckled out loud. What the hell was a Blue Tick Hound?

Jeff's email reinforced for me that we were at an impasse and had to find a way to get through it. Like Rich, Jeff was typically straight-forward, with no time for dramatics. But here he was referring to a "baying, slobbering Blue Tick Hound" and how if we did not "catch this critter," we would "die trying."

Perhaps Jeff hadn't had a good night's sleep when he sent that e-mail out, or perhaps he was just as aggravated as the rest of us that the lawyers were destroying the deal everyone had worked so hard for so many months to reach. Howard Glaser replied with his own email at 7:25 that morning: "I really thought you would go with the '2-minute warning' analogy. At least we are goal to go. We'll score today. Or that dog won't hunt."

Howard hit the nail on the head. In some ways, the lawyers were like dogs that refused to hunt. It doesn't matter what you do—some dogs just won't do it. My final interpretation of Jeff's and Howard's emails was that the lawyers simply could not finish the deal, so it was up to the three of them to complete it. Otherwise, the "hunt" was over. But I knew that none of them would allow the hunt to end before catching that "critter" to close the lease.

Things changed after the hounds were released. Rich, Howard, and Jeff took over the negotiations from the attorneys. Instead of a faceless attorney sending an email to the larger group arguing on behalf of his or her point, which ultimately resulted in more issues being created, the three of them went to work to resolve everything as soon as possible. Rich identified every open issue and sent an email to Jeff and Howard later that morning. They all agreed to participate in a previously scheduled conference call of attorneys at 1 o'clock that afternoon.

To say they "participated" in the call is an understatement. Listening in, it was apparent to me who was in charge. Every attorney had probably received their marching orders before the call from their respective general: Howard, Jeff, or Rich. Only the generals discussed how they were going to resolve each issue, unless it was necessary to bring in an attorney to discuss a particular point. During the call, many of the previously unresolvable issues were resolved, and it was quite apparent we were well on our way to bringing the chase to an end and closing the lease transaction.

Thankfully, whether they were generals or blue tick hounds, Rich Tobe, Howard Glaser, and Jeff Littmann could indeed hunt, as after that call, the lease transaction was back on track. In fact, most of the issues that the attorneys had grappled with for nearly two months were resolved within a couple of days. As a result, Jeff and Russ were able to present the final deal to the NFL's membership for its approval at its meetings on March 18, 2013. Approval was granted.

After ensuring everything related to the transaction was finalized, the attorneys sent out each document that needed to be signed to the approved signatories for each party: Russ Brandon for the Bills, Kenneth Adams for New York State, and me for Erie County. I received my set of documents during the first week of April, 2013. On Monday, April 8, we received email notification that Russ Brandon had signed the documents on behalf of the team the previous weekend. Because every document had to be signed many times over so that every party and their attorneys could have a set of fully signed set of original agreements, I then took to the long task of signing every signature page presented before me on behalf of Erie County.

I don't remember exactly how long it took me to sign all the documents, but it felt like a long time. When I finally set down my pen, I'm sure my face wore a huge smile—after sixteen months, our work was now complete.

On April 12, 2013, Ken Adams executed the full set of documents on behalf of New York State. Very shortly thereafter, the signature pages were exchanged by the parties, other requirements were met, and the transaction was closed. The lease deal was done, and our mission accomplished. The Bills would be legally required to play in Orchard Park for the next ten years. Though it took much longer than I had anticipated, we had done what we set out to do.

Epilogue

Much has occurred since the lease agreement was signed. However, following the closing of the transaction, two key dates proved all the work we put into the lease was not in vain: March 25, 2014, and September 9, 2014. March 25 was the day that Ralph Wilson, the only owner the Buffalo Bills had ever had, passed away at his home. September 9 was the day it was announced that Terry and Kim Pegula had entered into an agreement to purchase the team from Mr. Wilson's estate.

On March 25, several staff members and I were touring Ralph Wilson Stadium to check out how renovations were going. Russ Brandon was not on the tour, and I heard from one of the Bills' staff members on the tour that Mr. Wilson was not doing well. Satisfied with the progress of the renovations, our group headed back to the Rath Building.

I hadn't been back in my office for more than an hour when Jeff Littmann called Rich Tobe. I was told by Rich's secretary I should immediately go to his office and participate in a call. I walked in, and Jeff was talking to Rich via speaker phone, informing him of the passing of Mr. Wilson. Hearing Jeff's voice, it was apparent he was very emotional. On behalf of the community, I offered my condolences not only to Jeff and the Wilson family but to the entire Bills organization. Later that day, I spoke to Russ and reiterated my condolences to him and the team. It was a sad day for Bills Nation.

Following the call with Jeff, Rich and I sat down with senior staff, including my press team, to inform them of the news and prepare for the upcoming onslaught of media questions. We drafted a short statement, which I would put out on twitter as soon as the news of Mr.

Wilson's death was confirmed by the organization, and a longer one to be issued directly to the media, and then we waited for the team to officially confirm his death. When word of Mr. Wilson's passing became official, my press secretary Peter Anderson's phone would not stop ringing—every media outlet was calling to find out whether the team would now move.

I really had no intention of addressing the media that day. I was hoping to avoid talking about the lease and leaving the day for remembrance of Mr. Wilson. However, the questions from local, national, and even international media would not stop coming in, including one out-of-area outlet wanting me to comment on a rumor that the ten-year lease we negotiated had some secret provision allowing the team to move upon his death. So rather than talk to each outlet individually, Peter arranged for a press conference to be held later that afternoon in which all questions would be answered.

I opened the press conference reading my official statement of condolences and noted that "our community would not be the same without the Buffalo Bills. It is in some ways the glue that binds us together as Buffalonians and Western New Yorkers, and we have Mr. Wilson to thank for this. He was a man of great integrity who kept his word to our community." I ended my official comments by stating I had ordered all flags at County buildings to fly at half-staff until Mr. Wilson's funeral to honor him and his commitment to our community.

When I finished reading my prepared comments, I took questions from the media, and the first question from Buffalo Business First's Jim Fink was on what Mr. Wilson's death meant for the team's future in Buffalo and whether it would stay. I noted how Mr. Wilson always said he wanted to keep this team in Buffalo and that "he honored that commitment." He had also agreed to the ten-year lease, which he knew would in all likelihood outlive him.

Though I did not state it before the media, I was reminded of a comment Jeff Littmann said in passing to me at a football game in 2013 after we closed the transaction. To paraphrase Jeff, Mr. Wilson knew his time on earth was not long, and he had joked to Jeff that he "would probably be in the ground before the construction equipment" started digging into the ground for the renovation. While Mr. Wilson's joke was not true, as construction was progressing at a rapid pace prior to his death, Mr. Wilson knew he would not live to see the end of the latest lease. He entered into the lease agreement knowing full well that the provisions of the lease would be controlling regarding whoever purchased the team following his death.

I had put at the podium prior to the press conference my copy of the five-inch-wide bound copy of all the lease documents so that I could use it as a prop to remind media that the documents contained therein were still in effect. I then said in response to Jim's question, "The Buffalo Bills were here because of Mr. Wilson and will be here for many, many years to come because of the things Mr. Wilson has done recently by entering into the new lease agreement which ensures this team will be in Buffalo and Western New York."

The remainder of the twenty-minute press conference was spent basically answering the same question: whether the team would stay or move. I deferred all questions on issues related to Mr. Wilson's estate to the team and his attorneys. I also would not comment on a hypothetical sale of the team. I answered a question on Jim Kelly's battle against cancer, noting that cancer is a nondiscriminatory disease that can affect anyone, including my own brother the year before, and then wrapped up the press conference.

The other important date following the lease's closing was September 9, 2014, the date the estate of Ralph Wilson entered into a formal agreement to sell the team to Kim and Terry Pegula. Between those dates, there were so many rumors and innuendos regarding the sale of the team that I could write a whole other book on what actually occurred. In short, while the Pegulas did end up purchasing the team and have committed to keeping the Bills in Buffalo for as long as they own the team, there were many other prospective purchasers, and most of them had no intention of keeping the team in Buffalo.

Mr. Wilson's estate and the team required any prospective purchaser to sign a non-disclosure agreement before information on the team would be shared with the potential buyer. While I do not know how many prospective purchasers actually signed a non-disclosure agreement with the team and Mr. Wilson's estate, I was aware of approximately ten potential purchasers through various sources. Three of these possible purchasers were from the Los Angeles area, and two were from the Toronto area.

In the end, only three prospective purchasers submitted bids to purchase the team: the Pegulas, Donald Trump, and the "Toronto" group of Larry Tanenbaum, chairman of Maple Leaf Sports and Entertainment; Edward Rogers, chairman of Rogers Communications; and Jon Bon Jovi. When I heard that only three bids were submitted, and that the Pegulas had been chosen, I was pretty sure the lease's strong non-relocation clauses were the main reason for the limited number of bids.

My belief was confirmed when I spoke to Russ Brandon on the first game day following the Pegulas taking ownership of the team, a game against the rival New England Patriots. A big pregame event was scheduled for one of the grass practice fields north of the stadium, and I was invited to attend it with members of my staff. A tent covered many food stations, and members of the Bills staff were all waiting to meet the new owners. Kim and Terry came with their children, all wearing Bills' jerseys, and mingled about talking to everyone assembled. New England Patriots owner Robert Kraft came as well and presented Terry with a gift and welcomed him into the "club."

Russ was making his way around the event, and we talked for a few minutes about how happy everyone was and what the Pegulas ownership of the franchise would mean for the community. While Russ lost the title of chief executive officer to Terry Pegula, he was still the team's president and would be guiding the team's business operations for many years to come, at least as he anticipated. So it is fair to say Russ was in a very good mood that day.

Russ told me that many prospective out-of-area owners "kicked the tires of the team" but did not come close to placing a bid "because of the non-relocation agreement." We talked about possible bidders from Los Angeles, and he said "there were a few." He noted they all walked away when they realized they could not move the team until 2020 at the earliest. He said the strong non-relocation agreement, and especially the $400 million penalty provision, caused the vast majority of prospective bidders to walk away.

There is no doubt that one of the reasons the team is still in Buffalo is because of Kim and Terry Pegula. We are lucky to have such benefactors who care about the Bills, the Buffalo Sabres, and our community. However, it is also clear that another reason the team is still in Buffalo is the non-relocation provisions we demanded as part of the agreement.

There is no doubt in my mind that if the final lease did not contain such provisions there would have been many more bids submitted for the team, including from purchasers who intended to move the team to either Los Angeles or Toronto. It is possible some exceptionally wealthy billionaire hedge fund manager who wanted to move the team elsewhere could have been part of a bidding war to purchase the team and join one of the smallest clubs in the world—the owners of NFL football teams. Thankfully, we never had to witness that scenario take place because the ironclad non-relocation provisions, including being part of a separate agreement from the lease, ensured no one who intended to move the team would bid on it.

The team, our team, will be playing at New Era Field, as Ralph Wilson Stadium is now named, through the expiration of the lease in 2023. What happens afterward, whether they play at New Era Field or in a new stadium elsewhere (as sought by NFL Commissioner Roger Goodell), remains an open question. What is not in question is because of the hard work of many, the Bills will be known as the *Buffalo* Bills, and while it might not add up to a win in the NFL's standings, it is one of the biggest wins the community could have hoped for, at least until our Bills finally win the Super Bowl.

While the Bills are staying in Buffalo (or Orchard Park to be specific) for the foreseeable future, much has changed for the parties involved in the lease transaction—so much so that it's fitting to highlight the current status of many of the parties involved in the 2012 negotiations, some of whom will definitely not be participating in any future lease discussions.

New York State

Governor Andrew Cuomo was re-elected as New York's governor in 2014, and was easily re-elected to a third term in 2018. Governor Cuomo is the only governor during my lifetime to invest significant state resources in Buffalo and Erie County to address the decades of economic stagnation that plagued the region, including the signature "Buffalo Billion" investment to jump start the local economy. While many criticize the Buffalo Billion for various reasons, including how the contractor was chosen for a key solar project in Buffalo (more on that later), there can be no questioning the economic turnaround of the Buffalo–Niagara region during the past few years. In fact, the unemployment rate for the Buffalo–Niagara region for the month of July 2018 was the lowest it had been during any month during the prior eighteen years. I consider Governor Cuomo a friend, and I thank him for his continual investment of State resources into western New York. Working together, we have created the "New Buffalo" and the "New Erie County."

Lieutenant Governor Robert Duffy had a long and distinguished career in public service, first as a police officer in Rochester, New York, then police chief of the city of Rochester, then mayor of Rochester, and finally culminating in his election as New York's lieutenant governor in 2010. Duffy—or the "LG," as he was affectionately known—played a key role in the negotiations leading to the successful completion of the lease agreement, and I will be eternally grateful for his efforts. After one term as the lieutenant governor, Robert decided not to run for reelection in 2014, and since has been serving as the president and CEO of the Greater Rochester Chamber of Commerce.

Howard Glaser had always been known for being a fierce negotiator and close confidant of Governor Cuomo, and nothing I witnessed during the negotiation dented that reputation. I have a deep respect for Howard's abilities, and I know he served the people of New York well as the director of state operations. In June of 2014, Howard left the Cuomo administration and is now the Theodore Kheel Fellow for Transportation Policy at The Roosevelt House Public Policy Institute at Hunter College in New York City.

Joe Percoco was once among the most feared persons in New York as Governor Cuomo's executive secretary and "gatekeeper" to the governor. Today, Joe is a felon after being convicted in the U.S. District Court for the Southern District of New York on March 13, 2018, of three corruption charges related to his taking more than $300,000 from companies with business before the State. Once one of the most powerful people in New York, Joe was sentenced to six years in prison for the crimes he committed.

One of the foremost experts in the area of sports law, Irwin Raij is now the co-chair of the Sports Industry Group at the law firm of O'Melveny & Myers LLP.

There is no person of my generation I respect more in local or state government than John Maggiore. John is the consummate example of what a smart, ethical, and dedicated public servant should be. I have great respect for John's work and work ethic—so much so I have asked him to join my administration on multiple occasions. Unfortunately for me, but fortunately for the citizens of New York, John is dedicated to his work, and New York State is better for it. John is currently the policy director for Governor Andrew Cuomo.

Buffalo Bills

Other than the late Ralph Wilson's wife Mary Wilson, no one was closer to Mr. Wilson than Jeff Littmann. It was said by many in the Bills organization that Jeff was not just Mr. Wilson's chief confidant and financial guru, but that Mr. Wilson treated him like a son. Upon the sale of the team by the estate of Mr. Wilson to Terry and Kim Pegula, Jeff resigned his position as chief financial officer of the team and is now the chairman of the Board of Trustees of the Ralph C. Wilson, Jr. Foundation. The Ralph C. Wilson, Jr. Foundation was created following Mr. Wilson's death and is funded by the proceeds from the sale of the football team. The foundation is dedicated to improving the lives of the citizens of southeast Michigan, the home of Mr. Wilson, and western New York, the adopted home of Mr. Wilson. Since its formation in 2015, the foundation has donated millions of dollars to worthy causes in southeast Michigan and western New York.

After the sale of the team to the Pegulas, Russ Brandon contin-ued in the role as president of the Buffalo Bills, would eventually be named president of the Buffalo Sabres National Hockey League fran-chise (another sports team owned by Terry and Kim Pegula), and was also named president of Pegula Sports and Entertainment, LLC, by the Pegulas. However, on May 1, 2018, Russ resigned from all of his positions after a swirl of controversy erupted regarding a relationship Brandon may have had with an employee. While never confirmed, published media reports indicate Russ may have had an inappropriate relationship with a female subordinate employee. Suffice to say, whatever occurred was enough for the Pegulas to lose faith in Russ, leading to his resignation.

Lou Ciminelli and his firm LP Ciminelli were at the heart of many of the large construction projects in the western New York region for decades. In regards to the renovation of what was then Ralph Wilson Stadium, the Bills chose LP Ciminelli to be the construction manager of the project. LP Ciminelli is now out of business following the trial and July 12, 2018, conviction of Lou Ciminelli, with others, on federal charges of fraud and conspiracy to rig bids regarding the awarding of construction contracts for the massive "Riverbend" solar project in Buffalo, a project that now houses a Tesla solar roof product production facility. On December 3, 2018, Lou Ciminelli was sentenced to 28 months in a federal prison and ordered to pay a fine of at least $500,000 for the bid-rigging crimes he committed against the people of the State of New York.

While not parties to the lease transaction, Terry and Kim Pegula are still the owners of the Buffalo Bills and Buffalo Sabres, and have made significant multi-million-dollar investments in downtown Buffalo, including the construction and operation of "HarborCenter," a two-ice rink complex, training academy, and Marriot Hotel adjacent to Key Bank Arena, where the Sabres play. All discussions regarding the Buffalo Bills and where the team will play in the future will involve the Pegulas, discussions I can confirm have already started. As proof of their dedication to keeping the team in Buffalo, the Pegulas have invested more than $20 million of their own money into recent renovations at the stadium complex, including upgrades to the club seat restaurant and bar areas, and have announced another nearly $20 million investment to renovate the team's training complex. I consider my working relationship with Kim and Terry to be strong, as we discuss matters related to the team and their business interests multiple times a year either in person or through Bruce Popko, the chief operating officer of Pegula Sports and Entertainment. I look forward to having a long and productive relationship with the Pegulas in the future, especially when we finally organize a big celebration for the Bills winning the Super Bowl or the Sabres the Stanley Cup.

Erie County

I knew Rich Tobe had impressed Governor Cuomo and his staff with his work on the lease agreement—I just did not realize how much until early June 2015, when Rich walked into my office and told me he had been offered his dream job: to coordinate all upstate New York economic development for the Governor's Office. In effect, Rich was going to be the upstate New York economic development czar for the Cuomo Administration. In that role, Rich became the point person in determining how $1.5 billion dollars of state economic assistance would be spent in upstate regions, not including Buffalo (derisively though pretty much spot-on known as the "Upstate Hunger Games"). Following completion of that project, Rich led the governor's efforts to prod local governments to share services more effectively in an effort to reduce property taxes and has coordinated the State's efforts to properly prepare for the 2020 federal census. Currently, Rich serves as deputy director of state operations for Governor Cuomo.

Michael Siragusa is still the county attorney for Erie County.

Peter Anderson remains the press secretary for my administration.

After a very long career in public service, John Loffredo retired as Erie County's Commissioner of Public Service in January 2017. William Geary, the former Deputy Commissioner of Public Works for Highways, is now serving as Commissioner of Public Works.

Following Rich Tobe's resignation, I named Maria Whyte to be Deputy County Executive. I was very impressed with the work Maria did as Commissioner of Environment and Planning. Like Rich, I tasked Maria Whyte with focusing her daily efforts on growing our local economy, which she has done through her roles on various local agencies and as a partner with local businesses.

As for myself, I was reelected Erie County Executive in 2015, and it is my intention to run for reelection again in 2019. If I am given the privilege by the people of Erie County to serve a third term, I will once again lead the County's team in another lease negotiation with the Bills, considering the current lease expires in 2023.

Acknowledgments

Writing this book took much longer than I thought it would. I started writing it on April 7, 2014, completed the first draft on June 28, 2016, and edited it many times during the remainder of 2016 and through-out 2017, with final edits being completed on September 4, 2018. At various times I thought about ending the project as it was just too time-intensive to write while governing, then running for reelection for county executive in 2015, and then governing the county again. Erie County is geographically the same size as the state of Rhode Island and is larger in population than five states—South Dakota, North Dakota, Wyoming, Alaska, and Vermont—so getting the manuscript done was not a high priority compared to governing a county as large as Erie County. However, I did not want to turn over my notes, emails, and other documents to a ghost writer to finish it. I am glad I didn't do that because in writing this book I not only relived the process but was reminded of the good work performed by many, most of the time behind the scenes without any accolade, which led to the final lease.

As is apparent from the book, I owe a debt of gratitude to Rich Tobe for all his good work during the lease negotiations. Rich and I talked about the transaction from start to finish it seemed like every day, and while we both had many other activities to attend to daily, without his advice, steadying influence, and trusting relationship with Jeff Littmann, the final deal might have looked quite different. While I lost a deputy county executive when Rich Tobe left to join the Cuomo Administration, I know New York is a much better place for having Rich in such a key role.

The staff in the county attorney's office, starting with our county attorney Michael Siragusa, to assistant county attorneys Martin Polowy and Greg Kammerer, performed a great deal of behind-the-scenes work, especially as it pertained to hammering out security agreements for the stadium, and I thank them for their efforts.

Budget Director Robert Keating, as well as former Deputy Budget Director Tim Callan and Bob's staff, all performed admirably by providing updated analysis on the impact the various lease outcomes could have on the county's bottom line. I thank them for their good work.

As noted, after Rich Tobe left, I elevated Maria Whyte from commissioner of environment and planning to deputy county executive. One of the reasons I did so was because of the work she did to guide her staff, especially the office of Geographic Information Services (GIS), during the negotiation process. Maria, Deputy Commissioner Tom Dearing (whom I later promoted to commissioner and who has since retired), and Dale Morris of GIS all contributed to the final product.

When I lost Rich Tobe to the State, I also lost Liz Burakowski. She was offered a job and works as Rich's special assistant on upstate economic matters. She lived the entire lease negotiation process, and her hard work and dedication throughout the process helped to see it through.

Others from my administration played key roles and should be acknowledged and thanked. Peter Anderson and Mark Cornell each were left with the thankless task of rebuffing media requests for updates on lease negotiations, updates that were never forthcoming. My job would have been much harder if I'd had to deal with the media's persistent inquiries, and I thank Peter and Mark for their work.

Former Commissioner of Public Works John Loffredo and his staff worked very hard to take our plans for the renovation and make them a reality. Jesse Burnette from the Office of Equal Opportunity and Employment made certain that our minority and women business and worker goals were met. My secretary Martha "Marty" Taggart, Chief of Staff Jennifer Hibit, and former senior assistant Joe McMahon (who now serves as chief of staff to Town of Amherst Supervisor Brian Kulpa) somehow found a way to keep me sane throughout the process. They all deserve thanks.

I want to thank my family, my parents Charles and Janice, and my two brothers Robb and Kevin, as well as other close friends I had during the period of negotiating the lease and writing this book. Their perspective all helped during the entire process.

Thank you to Heather Novak and her daughter Nadia for all your love and support during these past two and a half years. Without your support it is doubtful I would have been able to finish this manuscript while I dealt with the myriad of issues, both good and bad, I faced as county executive. Thank you, Heather, for also being my sounding board on many of the ideas and initiatives I've implemented as executive during this period. Many of the accomplishments I've attained during this period are as much yours as mine.

Thank you to Maria Whyte for reading the first few chapters of the book and telling me it "did not stink," which helped me to see it through. I also want to thank Dan Meyer of my staff for reading my initial draft and offering grammatical and stylistic suggestions for the book, including Dan coming up with the idea for the book's title— "Beyond the Xs and Os." Thanks to all for your work.

Thank you to Professor Bruce Jackson for reading through the completed manuscript and offering a fair critique of the draft, as well as a number of recommendations. One of his suggestions was to employ an editor of the manuscript, and he recommended Woodrow "Woody" Brown. That was a great recommendation because Woody's edits did not significantly alter what I wrote, but strengthened the manuscript and made it less legalistic in tone. Thank you Woody for making the book better in the end.

Finally, thank you to the people of Erie County for giving me the privilege to serve as your county executive. Just like any job, there are good and bad days, but it truly is an honor to serve the people of our county, and I thank you for placing your trust in me to guide our community forward.

Index